## Praise for *All We Knew But Couldn't Say*

What you need to know about  how brilliantly Joanne Vannicola writes about mayhem and emotio that it's like becoming mesmerizeu ........ towards you. Becoming an actor may have been Joanne Vannicola's first step in avoiding the path of destructive forces heading her way — but it's her writing that feels like a storm contained. This is a story you won't soon forget.

— David Layton, award-winning author of *Motion Sickness*

Joanne Vannicola weaves a compelling narrative about hardship, survival, and resilience that reminds all of us about the enduring importance of forgiveness, family acceptance, and love.
    — Sarah Kate Ellis, president and CEO, GLAAD

Stark. Unflinchingly honest and filled with a type of determination that is seen in LGBTQ people who want more than just survival.
    — Roland Emmerich, director, producer

Joanne Vannicola's memoir is shocking, upsetting, and occasionally graphic, yet what sets it apart from other similar accounts is an under-lying sense of optimism. Out of despair there has emerged a beauti-fully written account, where the author has not only come through the tribulations of her early life, but become a leading voice for the overlooked and the marginalized. I cannot recommend it enough.
    — Linda Riley, publisher, DIVA Magazine

In this moving memoir, Joanne Vannicola writes herself — and so many of us who have experienced oppression and trauma — onto the page. As a writer, I enjoyed her beautiful, well-paced, and evoc-ative storytelling. As a therapist and survivor, I found myself paus-ing and nodding as she articulated so well her deep and layered understandings of trauma and marginalization. Throughout, I found myself rooting for and cheering on the young girl, actor, activist, and woman of this story.

— Farzana Doctor, author

This frank, sometimes harrowing, always inspiring memoir should be mandatory reading for all — for those afraid of being true to themselves or anyone who needs a hero that demonstrates what personal courage and determination can do. PLEASE READ THIS BOOK!

— Colin Mochrie, actor, comedian

I am completely gutted by reading Joanne's beautifully penned heart-wrenching memoir.... Raw, unflinching, brave, and important, it makes me grateful to know that a voice with this power and honesty is sharing her truth with us all.

— Cynthia Dale, actor

From her abusive parents and a harrowingly self-destructive adolescence to against-all-odds success as a performer, we anxiously cheer on that spark of joy in Joanne that not only refuses to be snuffed but flourishes to awareness and grace. I tore through this book in a fury, astounded by her resilience and inspired by her unerring belief in the power of love.

— Wendy Crewson, actor

A story fit for this time and the landscape of our culture, incredibly raw, moving, and honest. Joanne has survived so much and come out triumphant. A book worth reading.

— Denys Arcand, Oscar-winning director

Joanne writes the way she lives, with heart and hope and honesty. A must read.

— Helen Shaver, actor

# All We Knew But Couldn't Say

# All We

Joanne Vannicola

# Knew But

# Couldn't

# Say

DUNDURN
TORONTO

Cover images: Composite by David Drummond. House: istock.com/jenysarwar; Sky: istock.com/Jasmina007; Girl: Shutterstock.com/MariaRoldanPazos
Printer: Webcom, a division of Marquis Book Printing Inc.

**Library and Archives Canada Cataloguing in Publication**

Title: All we knew but couldn't say / Joanne Vannicola.
Other titles: All we knew but could not say
Names: Vannicola, Joanne, 1968- author.
Identifiers: Canadiana (print) 20190075805 | Canadiana (ebook) 20190075961 | ISBN 9781459744226 (softcover) | ISBN 9781459744233 (PDF) | ISBN 9781459744240 (EPUB)
Subjects: LCSH: Vannicola, Joanne, 1968- | LCSH: Television actors and actresses—Canada—Biography. | LCSH: Motion picture actors and actresses—Canada—Biography. | LCSH: Mothers and daughters—Canada—Biography. | LCGFT: Autobiographies.
Classification: LCC PN2308.V36 A3 2019 | DDC 791.4502/8092—dc23

1   2   3   4   5      23   22   21   20   19

  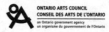

We acknowledge the support of the **Canada Council for the Arts**, which last year invested $153 million to bring the arts to Canadians throughout the country, and the **Ontario Arts Council** for our publishing program. We also acknowledge the financial support of the **Government of Ontario**, through the **Ontario Book Publishing Tax Credit** and **Ontario Creates**, and the **Government of Canada**.

Nous remercions le **Conseil des arts du Canada** de son soutien. L'an dernier, le Conseil a investi 153 millions de dollars pour mettre de l'art dans la vie des Canadiennes et des Canadiens de tout le pays.

VISIT US AT

dundurn.com | @dundurnpress | dundurnpress | dundurnpress

Dundurn
3 Church Street, Suite 500
Toronto, Ontario, Canada
M5E 1M2

*For my siblings.*

*In memory of Steffin Light and baby Joshua.*

*For anyone who has ever been hurt or marginalized, has suffered violence, or has felt like they don't belong, and for all survivors of child abuse or systemic violence. This book is also for all women and LGBTQ2+ people who need an ally and who need to see themselves in the stories they consume.*

# Walking Through Glass

PART ONE

# CHAPTER ONE

## 2002 — Princess Margaret Hospital

I NEVER KNOW what condition she'll be in when I arrive at the hospital — if she'll be lucid, rambling, awake, sleeping, in an altered state, or maybe even gone. Dead.

I wait, though, finishing my cigarette outside, squatting on the ground. My fingertips yellowed with nicotine. The skin chewed. The sky scattered and uncertain as if the spring sun might disappear and a storm might crash in. I exhale and stroke an exposed patch of grass as if it were the fur of a sleeping cat.

"Are you okay?" asks a woman.

I squint, shield my eyes, and look up from her stiletto heels to her bold red lips. Everything perfect and in place.

"My mother is dying," I say.

"I'm sorry," she says softly before walking away.

I stand up, squash my cigarette with my shoe, cross the street, and go through the revolving glass doors of Princess Margaret, Toronto's renowned cancer hospital. I wait for the elevator, pop peppermint gum into my mouth, fish my shades from my pocket, and push them on, covering the dark circles around my eyes.

The elevator is crammed with gowned patients clutching their IV poles, hospital staff, and fellow visitors. Some are here for those in the beginning stages of the disease, the newly diagnosed who are in treatment or having surgery. Then there are people like me, the dishevelled and overtired, the ones on constant duty, hurrying to the bathroom or stealing away for a quick smoke, afraid to miss the end.

It takes forever to get to the seventeenth floor: the palliative care ward. My sisters are outside our mother's room talking in whispers. My brother, Diego, is at home sleeping. We're on rotating shifts. My sisters, Sadie and Lou, have travelled from Montreal and Vancouver to say their goodbyes; yes, even Sadie, who was taken by the Children's Aid so many years ago, the day the rest of us were inexplicably left behind.

Mother slips in and out of consciousness, almost in a coma, her body bruised from multiple needles and the morphine drip. Her eyes are glassy, hollow. She is uncommunicative, the way my sisters like it. They don't want to talk or listen; they have never believed a word she said anyway. Lou refused to even come to Toronto unless I was certain Mother was dying.

It was winter when my mother was admitted. I didn't know then how long was left. Weeks? Months? I only knew she was declining, and unlike my sisters, I had questions that needed answering.

I walk into her room. Her bare feet are exposed, the skin like cracked mud under a hot sun. I should apply cream but am afraid to touch them. I am thirty-three years old, but my insides still revolt when I get close to her. The need to feel separate is so big, so old. So immediate.

I ignore her parched feet, busying myself with the messy counter beside her bed while I formulate the first question.

"Do you want to finally *talk*?" I stare at her.

"Not yet," she says and stares back.

I wipe the counter and rearrange the clutter: the box of Kleenex, the water jug, three Styrofoam cups, juice from breakfast. I throw out used tissues. I try again.

"Why did you marry him?" I ask. "Why Dad?"

"Because I had to," she answers. She grabs the remote and turns on the extendable tiny television that stretches out from the wall like the arm of a crane. "The new kids are so good," she says after finding a figure-skating competition. "That boy Sandhu, he can dance too...."

"But why? Was it because you were pregnant with Sadie?"

She pauses as if the answer is lost to her. I've seen it before, this vacancy, how she fumbles, makes things up she doesn't know, avoids reality.

"I think so...." Mother says, her voice stuck somewhere in her throat.

"You think so or you know so?"

"I don't know.... I ... well, your grandfather wanted me to marry your father." She turns off the television and shoves it away from her bed.

I actually know the real story, but not from my mother. From Diego, who told me years ago, after he had gone with Mother to a therapy session.

Mother was the youngest girl out of seven children: the "chosen" one, raped by her father. She told people, but no one believed her. I did. The moment Diego told me, I knew it was true. It was the only thing that made sense. A piece of her was broken long before any of us came along.

"And I loved your father," she interjects before I can say anything more. "I loved him. Isn't that enough?" She covers herself with the thin green hospital blanket.

It isn't. Because it isn't true. It can't be. He was a brute; she was a girl. What was to love?

When I was young, I obsessively asked her why she married my dad. He was terrifying, and even at the age of eight, I couldn't understand why she'd married him.

She would always say the same thing: "Because I loved him." Then she would throw up her arms to shut me up, as if she thought I could believe her. It was the most insane thing I had ever heard.

She interrupts my thoughts. "I want to speak with all my children." Her demeanour is imperious. "I forgive you all."

"What did you say?" I turn to her, feeling nauseous, dizzy almost. After everything she has done, she forgives *us*?

"And what do you forgive your children for? What have your children done to you that requires your forgiveness?" My voice is low, measured.

She stares at me without answering, fidgets with her bedding. Her voice changes, becomes childlike. "Do you forgive me?"

"I don't really know, but I know I won't forget."

I leave then, rush out, trying to stop the flood of memories. The dam breaks and I spend the night spinning backward, through my father's violence and my mother's collusion. And through something else, something hard to accept or talk about even now: how my mother touched me, and how I knew, even when I was a little girl, that it was wrong.

But I go back the next day, and she stares at me vulnerably from her bed. "I'm afraid of losing my hair."

I am sitting as far away from her as I can. The hospital room isn't big enough for the two of us. No room is big enough for the two of us.

"I don't know if I can handle seeing it fall out in chunks. I'm scared."

"Are you?" I ask. I don't want to take care of her. The very thought inspires rage. She takes up so much space, even physical space, and the room is small, making her seem larger somehow, as if I were still eight. I can't cope with her fear, so instead I focus on her hair, which will fall out from the last-ditch effort to prolong her life with chemotherapy.

"I can shave your head."

"Do you think that would help?" She looks at me hopefully, trying to find a way into my heart.

I find a cheap blue plastic razor and hold it up to Mother's head of curls while she sits up in her hospital bed.

"You're sure you trust me with this thing?" I ask, ready to shave her.

I hate her vulnerability and recall childhood fantasies when I wished her dead, when I hoped the plane would crash or the car would go off a cliff, her heart would stop or she would slip on the ice some winter night and crack her skull.

But here she is powerless, afraid of losing her long, luscious hair.

My mother always worked so hard on her appearance, trying to compensate for her weight: her 350 to 400 pounds. A gifted seamstress, she made her own clothes: wide tops and dresses in floral patterns, stripes, or paisley, in pinks and purples, blues and greens, in velour or velvet for special events or shows. She manicured her nails, painted her face, and coloured her hair — her beautiful, luscious hair. She permed it, straightened it, blow-dried it, curled it, always trying the newest style. Her hair was her armour, her confidence. It let her go out into the world, hiding her vulnerability and her monsters.

"I think I need to cut it first. It's too long to shave."

We are silent as I put white towels around her neck. I cut her hair, almost taken aback by how soft it is. I apply shaving cream and carefully move her head while the sharp blade scrapes against her scalp.

Shaving her head turns out to be a very intimate act. It is the closest I've been to her in over fifteen years. The only sounds come from the hall, where nurses congregate at their station, laughing or complaining, where buzzers sound, where patients shuffle by, where visitors walk, catching glimpses as I angle around earlobes and more of my mother's flesh becomes visible.

I pat her head dry. She is raw. Exposed. And so am I.

It's hard to hate when someone is dying.

I didn't always hate my mother.

Some of my earliest memories are good: tap shows and costumes, music and time steps. I was three years old when the lessons began. Luaus where my sister Lou and I performed Hawaiian dances with bamboo sticks and balls on a string, wearing grass skirts and floral tops. Tap and jazz shows. Trophies and competitions. Gymnastics and figure skating. Roller-skating lessons, partnered with a boy my age, rolling around in circles doing figure eights on wheels under disco balls in roller rinks. My mother wanted something for me. She wanted something for herself.

But in the end, it was the theatre and acting that would take root, where I would excel and live the dreams I thought were mine. They weren't. They were hers; yet, in the end, she didn't share in them. For fifteen years I was estranged from my mother, couldn't bear to be near her. She wasn't there in 1991 when I won my Emmy for *Maggie's Secret*, and she wasn't there in 1993 when I debuted at the Toronto International Film Festival with *Love and Human Remains*, directed by legendary Québécois director Denys Arcand. She wasn't there for most of my triumphs and, God knows, was never there for my disasters, when I needed — really needed — a mother.

# CHAPTER TWO

## 1973

CHILDREN IN COSTUMES and leotards were scattered inside and outside of the studio in a rundown area of Montreal. Dozens of shiny steel-toed shoes were reflected in the large mirrored wall. I learned to shuffle and triple-time step here in Miss Kristy's class. I fell in love with both her and the ability to make music with my feet. I was excited about dance, movement, about being alive. Miss Kristy planted a tiny seed and music filled a space inside that I hadn't really known existed until I met her and learned to tap. It was mixed up with love, drums, swing, jazz, blues, rock and roll, time steps, metronomes, and Miss Kristy hugs.

My mother also signed me up for drama lessons at a local children's theatre. I loved that more than anything: the land of make-believe was a perfect universe for a child like me. And it was the same for my mother, who had a certain twinkle in her eye when I was on the stage or when music played or when leather shoes pointed, tapped, or drummed. Mother's escape was the same as mine, only she experienced it vicariously through me and my sister Lou. If she could have worn the tap shoes she would have, but she could only be an observer. She knew the moves: pirouette, flap, Buffalo, and time steps. My mother knew the language of dance. This was our shared love, our point of connection. Everything else was chaos.

"Let's hurry and get going, girls," Mother said, swinging her arms at us to get us into the car. She wore one of the floral dresses that covered her rolls of fat, and smelled of Chanel perfume and talcum powder mixed with sweat. Her long, dark hair was made shorter by her accordion perm, but in the shuffle as we carried our belongings to the car, it became stringy and wet.

Sadie, my eldest sister, was fourteen, and like twelve-year-old Diego, she was at school. Lou was ten, and we were kept home to help pack the car.

Sadie had big green eyes and a cackle of a laugh. Diego had a Mick Jagger pout. Lou had chipped front teeth and freckles. I was skinny and quick, always watching over my shoulder, on the lookout for larger people, especially my father. He could make a child believe the devil was real.

We were escaping our father, dismantling our home while he was at work, taking only essentials and keepsakes. I was four years old the day we left him.

We raced around, carrying out our prized possessions and jamming the car with pots and pans, bedding, clothes, food, pharmaceuticals, photograph albums, tap and jazz shoes — anything we could cram into that one load.

My mother fumbled to get the key into the ignition. We held our breath until she managed to pull away from the curb. I looked through the back window to say goodbye to all I had ever known, but it was too late. We had already turned the corner. No time for goodbyes.

"He won't be back. I promise," my mother said with determination, sweat pouring down her face as she drove. Lou didn't speak, just stared at my mother with a type of hopeful uncertainty: a girl who demanded the truth, a big-mouthed older sister who wasn't keen on smiling, who had little to smile about.

What we all felt that morning was panic mixed with excitement over escape. In my four years of life, I had learned to survive despite a constant level of fear.

We left a street lined with yards and trees, where children played on the merry-go-round and baseball diamond in the park across from our house, and entered a block with no grass, just rows of townhouses and street lights, a working-class area. Houses were small, attached. Everything looked the same all the way up the block: rows and rows of tiny spaces filled with people living inside a grey world.

We didn't say anything when Mother told us that our father wouldn't be back. I remember counting in my own head — counting the stop lights, green lights, red lights — and holding on to Lou for dear life in the car, in a panic that we would be found, that somehow he could see and would know where we were, and if he found us there would be hell to pay.

We came to know our new neighbours and found places to play, found parks and abandoned houses to explore or get lost in that spring. I turned five years old in July, and our new friends gathered for the first birthday party I would remember.

"Happy birthday!" The room erupted after a vanilla-frosted cake was placed before me at the kitchen table.

"Make a wish, Joanne," Mother said.

A little boy named Bobby stuck his finger out to scoop up some icing before his mother swatted his arm away. There were mothers and children from the grey buildings piled into our apartment, women wearing polyester paisley dresses with fake jewellery, beehives, and buns, and children with shorts, sneakers, and food-covered faces.

"Cake! Cake! Cake!" the other children chanted. Lou put Glenn Miller on the record player and the mothers erupted when they heard "Chattanooga Choo Choo," singing along to it and pouring wine into plastic cups while we ate seconds of cake. I wondered if we had become like the Partridge Family, all giddy and sweet like their theme song, "Come On Get Happy."

We played openly and made noise at the dinner table and ran around if we felt like it. Diego was usually out getting into no good with other boys on the block. He always seemed absent. Even though he lived with us, he felt separate. Perhaps it was that he was so much older than I was, but in truth I think it was because he was a boy, and a boy in a Catholic Italian family had a much longer leash.

We girls spent a lot of time together. We constantly dared our mother to see if she would punish us for being naughty. My Crayolas found their way onto the white mat of a painting on the wall. Sweets were brought to the dining table before we finished the food on our plates. Sadie cursed outright and smelled like tobacco. I screamed at the top of my lungs as a new exercise, goaded and pushed to see if Mother would crack or smack me. She tried once, but I ran around and jumped over furniture and she gave up. Mostly she didn't do much, just stared with a strange numbness when she couldn't make us stop and no amount of yelling would do.

Without our father, our muscles relaxed and we were not on constant alert anymore, no longer hard-wired to scan for danger. It had taken weeks for my body to learn this new feeling, and I wasn't sure if I should trust it.

"Joanne. Come on, it's your move," Lou called out from upstairs.

The skim-milk-powder man had arrived to show our mother how to make milk from a package. He stood in our kitchen mixing water and powdered milk in a bowl, trying to get her to buy it.

"Cheaper than milk and will last a whole lot longer. Just pennies a packet," he explained as he pushed his crinkled shirt into his pants over and over again. He shifted back and forth from one foot to the other while Mother leaned against the counter and nodded her head up and down delicately — though she was hardly delicate — trying to seem interested while he droned on and on about powdered food. She had been struggling to feed us. When we first moved in it was chaotic and messy, almost daring, like the universe was testing us all to see if we could survive in this unkempt and sparsely furnished house without a father, without money. I liked it.

I ran upstairs to Lou and Sadie in the bedroom we shared. There were only three rooms: one for Diego, one for our mother, and one for us. Sadie was reading a magazine with David Cassidy's face on the front. She flipped through the pages, ignoring Lou and me. Lou sat on the floor in front of one of my birthday gifts, the game Operation, with her bag of barbecue chips ripped open and the radio playing. The window was covered with half a sheet tacked up, and our unmade mattresses were on the floor. I dropped down on my bed, grabbed the tweezers attached to the red wire, and tried to get the Toe Jam piece out of the foot.

"Lou, can milk be the same as when it comes out of a cow if it comes from a packet?"

The game's buzzer went off. Lou and I jumped while Sadie muttered "Jesus Christ" and then went back to reading.

Lou snatched the tweezers from me. "I don't know. I suppose if it tastes okay then it might be the same as real milk."

"So how come we didn't have powder before?" I asked.

"Who cares? We had Ding Dong before," Lou said.

"What's Ding Dong?"

"Dad."

All three of us burst into fits of laughter and chips fell to the floor. Lou got up to turn up the volume on the radio, where Elton

John's "Goodbye Yellow Brick Road" was playing. We both stood up and waved our arms around in the air like branches to the melancholic sounds. I did my best to imitate her. I could still hear the whir of the machine downstairs where the grown-ups were making milk.

"Are we going to have to eat food from a packet?" I asked Lou, tugging at her shirt as she sang along. "Lou. Lou!"

"What? Why you always gotta ask stupid questions?" Lou closed her eyes, trying to catch up with the lyrics. I sat down and stared at her waving around like a squid, then laughed.

"Whatcha laughing about?" Lou asked.

"Ding Dong," I said, and all three of us fell into hysterics.

"Girls," Mother called from downstairs, but we ignored her. "Turn down the music and come downstairs.... Do you hear me?" Mother shouted. "I want you to try the milk."

Just before Lou and I reached the bottom step, we heard the banging at the front door.

*Bang. Bang. Bang.*

"Open the door!" shouted the voice on the other side. I knew who it was. We all did. We froze. I stood beside Lou. The skim-milk-powder man stayed in the kitchen, and Mother walked over to open the door. She didn't look at us, but hesitated for a moment, her hand hovering above the doorknob. Lou squeezed my hand. My breath stuck in my chest. I heard the click of the unlocking door.

He stood in the rain with the thunder crashing around him, wearing his dirty work clothes, hard hat, and Kodiak boots after a day of constructing new houses for people to live in. Ours instantly fell apart.

Lou ran upstairs and I followed as Dad screamed at the skim-milk-powder man to get out of the house. Sadie wasn't reading anymore; she was facing the wall under a blanket with her back toward us, as if she were asleep. Lou and I instinctively cleaned, putting the game pieces away, the chips. There was yelling and smashing. Dad was throwing things and calling Mother a bitch.

Mother shouted, "Stop! Stop it! Stop …" until all that was left was the sound of the rain on the roof, the drums of thunder, and the wild flashes of light across the windows.

I stood in front of our closed door and listened. Sadie kept her face to the wall. Lou took my hand and gently guided me toward my bed while humming a tune.

I wiped my nose and eyes on my sleeve and took a deep breath. The trembling returned in my chest. Lou grabbed a bag of elastics from the dresser drawer and started to braid my hair, not one or two, but as many tiny little braids as she could twist on my head. We sat for hours like monkeys in a tree, grooming hair, comforting, and resting in each other's arms while the moon rose and the room went dark.

The thunder seemed to be permanently present inside that apartment after our father came back, after our failed escape. The very walls seemed to inspire a type of doom; even our new rescue animals were not immune, our cat, Candy, and our dog, Velvet.

Poor creatures. That they had landed in our home was a tragedy. Our cat had a litter of kittens, and my favourite kitten was smothered by her mother and lay dead beneath her. I couldn't stop wailing. Sick of my screaming, my father went upstairs with a shovel and killed the remaining kittens.

I don't remember the feeling, but it was something like white noise — like something had taken over my body and had frozen it in time, like a piece of me broke. Up until that point, I didn't know death, didn't know a mother cat could smother her baby, that my father could kill the rest out of rage, that life could be permanently erased. And it happened because I cried.

In my thirties, I was asked, "But you must have had good times, good memories?"

There were, only the bad ones were so bad I couldn't quite hang on to the good.

# CHAPTER THREE

ENGLISH-SPEAKING FAMILIES were packing their cars and leaving Montreal in droves during the language conflicts between French and English Quebecers in the 1970s. Children had to prove what language they spoke and businesses had to adopt French as their official language. Eventually that would change, too, but not before many people left.

We, however, stayed. All we left were the row houses when I was five for a house on the West Island, in Pierrefonds, with two storeys and a yard out back and a large wooden deck with old appliances sitting under it — stoves and a freezer that could be used for great games of make-believe. Fragrant lilac trees filled our senses and the big beautiful pine, birch, and maple trees had high branches that seemed as if they could touch the sky. The walls in the house were painted bright, light colours: oranges and yellows.

We were on a cul-de-sac with a mound of grass in the centre and evenly mowed lawns around us. Every house had a garage, even ours, and that was where our father stored his tools, converting it into a workshop.

It was as if we had never escaped him. We all pretended and acted like it had never happened and tried to blend in with the other families on the block, where life seemed so normal, where children played red light/green light, hide-and-seek, and tag until dark. Flowers bloomed, and neighbours had above-ground pools, basketball nets, and pets and doghouses. We rode bicycles with banana seats and bells.

I found a hiding place under the front porch and would slide under the concrete deck through a small crevice. I brought my favourite toys under the porch, my red plastic Close 'n Play phonograph-record player, and my favourite 45s. Music was my salvation.

Sadie, Lou, and I listened to music together regularly when our parents were out — the Beatles, Elvis, Rod Stewart. On one occasion, Sadie and Lou sang and jiggled on the couch side by side to a Janis Joplin LP, snapping their fingers and swinging their heads in unison. I was lying on the carpeted floor with my eyes closed, communicating with Joplin's spirit. I did this with all the dead singers we listened to, certain I could communicate with "famous ghosts."

When our parents were gone, it was like the black and white of life switched to colour, and we made as much noise as we could, listened to music, and ran about unreserved.

One day, Sadie suggested we make hot chocolate and sandwiches. Lou and I shouted our approval and scrambled to the kitchen. Lou grabbed the food out of the fridge and I passed it to Sadie. The smell of cheese, bread, and chocolate drifted through the air. I mixed the powdered chocolate with milk on the stove, standing on a chair. When everything was ready, we sat down at the kitchen table to eat and devoured our food as quickly as we'd made it. Our pace was always frantic, getting in as much unadulterated sister time as possible, cramming in pleasure, then wiping it away. We carried our plates to the sink, knowing not to leave any visible crumbs. We placed our mugs on the counter, washed the table, and left our little yellow kitchen, content that we had covered up our mess.

"We're home!" yelled our mother that evening after the front door opened. Our parents thumped up the stairs above us.

We were in the basement watching *The Bionic Woman* on our black-and-white television with the rabbit ears on top. We turned down the volume.

"Sadie, Lou, Joanne, Diego, did you hear me? Get up here now!" Mother said in a tone of voice not to be ignored. We knew the drill. My body felt like it had just doubled in size, so heavy, and every step up from the basement to our parents was like going against the current. If there was a sixth sense in our house, it was fear.

"Where's your brother?"

"He's been out all day," Sadie said as we filed into the kitchen.

"Sit down. We want to talk to you," Mother said, her face calm, quiet. "Who left the mess?" Mother had her "going out" makeup on: thick blush, blue eyeshadow above her green eyes, and bright red lipstick. She was wearing one of her handmade dresses. She made some of our clothes, too, because it cost less than buying new from the local Zellers, especially dress-up clothes for weddings or church services. She was jiggly and soft, with arms as round as loaves of bread.

"Who left the mess?" she asked again, arms up, staring at us calmly while our father towered above us, with tight lips, tornado eyes, large fists clenched, and popped blue veins under his skin as he paced. His face was balled up with rage, like a trapped wild animal. I looked around. The place was spotless. But then I saw them — the three mugs on the kitchen counter.

It was quiet. None of us looked at each other; we were still, half breathing, the smell of Mother's powder mixed with our fear and the sound of my father's feet pacing behind us, *boom, boom, boom.*

"I did it," Sadie finally said after an agonizing silence.

Dad grabbed Sadie. Lou ran out of the kitchen to get away and I stood up. Dad punched Sadie, then dragged her to the floor, hitting her and hitting her. She screamed while I looked at my mother, hoping she would make it stop. Mother just watched, in a trance with no expression. She pulled me into her, holding me tight. Sadie was on the floor taking it for all of us, and I couldn't tell anymore if it was her or me that was screaming. I floated, looked out at a sea of red. It was Sadie's blood, flowing from her nose. She cradled her arm and tried to shelter her face from the blows that never seemed to end.

This was when I learned the next horrible lesson of our home — maybe the worst. That our mother was not interested in saving us. She had called us up to "talk," wanted to know who had left the "mess," and waited patiently until he blew. She wound him up like a music box and would not let me run, forcing me to witness the brutality while she squeezed and gripped my small frame.

Sadie was forbidden to leave her room the following day. She wasn't allowed to eat, talk on the phone, or go to school. I snuck down to her room, brought her some dry cereal and my plastic fur-covered black panther for company. Her room smelled of musty urine. She was curled up, soft and exposed like a crustacean without a shell. I kissed her wet cheek and then went to school.

It was impossible to concentrate at school. I was guilty for being silent while Sadie took the beating. It took everything in me to act like the other children, who played tag or hopscotch, answered questions in class, or raised their hands to read out loud from picture books before the end of the day. I could only stare, physically there but nowhere near present.

When I got home from school, Sadie asked me to sneak her something to eat.

I scampered up the stairs and into the kitchen. Mother was in the dining room making lasagna, rolling out the dough and cranking noodles through the metal machine, flour puffing into a cloud in the air, with the smell of tomato sauce and onions simmering on the stove in large lidded pots. Making lasagna just like nothing had happened.

I was quiet at the dinner table and managed to tuck a piece of white crusty bread under my shirt. Lou and I stared at each other sideways while Diego and Mother ate quietly and my father scooped a heap of noodles and cheese into his mouth.

Dad had little tenderness; nothing about him was soft, everything sharp, from his tongue to his fist. He seemed almost giant-sized, only he wasn't round like my mother, just hard and mean, with a fake eye that never moved, frozen like his heart. Sometimes I liked to stare at his fake eye to see if it might magically move or follow me, but it never did.

He ate his meal in silence, chewed his food, grunted and burped. I left when the meal was done, carried my dish to the sink, then disappeared. Sadie was on her bed staring at the wood-panelled wall in a trance, her lips slightly open as she breathed in and out, the only real sign that she was still inside herself. I wasn't sure what it was that made people stare that way, if it was sadness, loneliness, or hunger. My mother had that look in her eyes sometimes, too. Usually, with Mother, it was when she didn't think I was looking or when she ate too much.

Mother always snuck food while she cooked. She ate bread lathered in butter or smothered in sauces, used fingers for forks, ate mouthfuls of cooked and baked goods and chocolates, and gulped cans of Pepsi to wash it all down, hand over mouth as she chewed and swallowed as if in a race, looking around before she would wipe food or sweat from her face with sighs and groans.

That night, Sadie was screaming again. Dad hadn't finished the beating. Smashing and bashing came from the basement, and Lou covered her head with a pillow while I got out and paced by her bedside.

I paced back and forth on the spot, one foot to the next as if I were standing on hot stones, my breath shallow, my flannel Cookie Monster pyjamas wet with the sweat of panic. I started to cry. Lou lifted her blanket up to expose her face, inviting me into her bed and her arms.

I crawled in and put my head on Lou's pillow, facing her, and grabbed her arm. If there had been a way to hide inside of her, I would have done it. If she hadn't curled around me like a mother bird, I would have spun away.

I heard my mother's voice outside the door asking us what was going on. I said I was thirsty and a minute later she was in our room with a glass of milk.

"You should be asleep by now." She held the glass for me while I drank.

"Okay, Mommy."

"Good night." She smiled after she kissed my cheek tenderly, like nothing was wrong.

# CHAPTER FOUR

A FEW DAYS LATER, I ran home after school and opened Sadie's bedroom door, but she wasn't there. Her bed was empty, her blankets strewn on the floor. I ran upstairs to find my mother.

"Sadie went to school this morning and said some things she shouldn't have. A social worker came by this afternoon to tell me that Sadie won't be coming back."

I didn't know what a social worker was, but to my child's mind it wasn't good. They stole my sister, just took her, and worse, my mother was acting as if she'd lost a glove or scarf. I couldn't bear to stay near her, so I went to my room and started jumping from my bed to Lou's bed, back and forth, while looking out of the window, hoping I might see Sadie, that it might be a mistake or a lie. Lou came in the room while I was frantically leaping.

"They took her, Lou! She went to school and something happened and someone came here to talk to Mother and now Sadie is gone."

"Who took her?" Lou asked, running out of the room.

I jumped off the bed, found a crayon, and furiously scribbled on some paper, and all I could think to do was scream all the obscenities Sadie had taught me. "Bastard. Cocksucker. Fuck face."

Lou came back in, without answers. The crayon dropped from my hand to the floor; Lou bent down to pick it up and replaced it in the Crayola box. "Do you want to push our beds together so we can make a giant bed?" she asked.

I nodded yes and we moved the night table that sat between our beds, then pushed them together to form a giant mattress. I curled into Lou while she held on to me. Her face was wet but I didn't say anything. Neither of us spoke.

Sadie was my foundation, even if it was Lou and I who found her food when she was hungry or tried to make her laugh when she was scared or lonely. She protected us. We were allies, the parts that made a whole, and Sadie was the biggest part; without her it was just Lou and I … and Diego, but he didn't count. And we weren't enough. It was Sadie who played the albums on the record player. Sadie who spoke up when we were too afraid, Sadie who made the big-girl decisions when we were on the bus or in the park, Sadie who held my hand when we crossed the street.

No one from social services ever came to the house, or at least never came when I was there. No one spoke to me or to Lou, and I was glad. At the time I was afraid of being taken, too. Disappearing without a trace. The only lesson I learned from Sadie's absence was to keep my mouth shut, to never tell on my parents, even when I was the victim.

"Joanna, come now." Dad came home from work with a mud-caked face, smelling of sawdust and grease, in his Kodiak boots, gloves, helmet, and soot-covered overalls with a weathered leather belt that held his hammer, screwdrivers, and nails. "Boots."

"Boots" meant I had to remove his boots.

"We eat?" meant "When is supper going to be on the table?" Dad had other words, the words he used to call his girls — *whore, bitch, cockroach.*

In the mornings my father would stand over the sink in freshly laundered coveralls that Mother would clean every night. He would open the mirrored medicine cabinet and pull out from the little shelf a case that held his glass eye. He would stretch his eyelid open with his fingers to expose the red veins and the gaping hole in his face, like invisible murky water at the bottom of a lake miraculously made visible. He would insert the glass eye, green eyeball perfectly centred. He'd lost his eye with one swift smash in the face with the forked part of a hammer at work. The one-eye shift never stopped fascinating me, the perfect focal point when looking at him.

When we drove, sometimes he would veer too far to one side of the road and my mother would gasp and scream, "Are you trying to kill us?"

He would giggle and we would giggle back. He thought dangerous driving was funny. One day he got into an accident and the car swerved and did complete circles in the snowy road until it landed in a ditch. I wasn't in the car and no one was hurt, but when he saw me, he said, "You would have had so much fun. The car went two time circle and boom!"

I could tell Mother thought he was an idiot. Kids know these things. Who talks about having fun in a car accident?

"I swear if you could only get your brains examined," Mother said under her breath while drying her hands with a kitchen towel by the stove. Dad smiled, bounced me on his leg, like a child himself, a child my own age delighting in spins and whirls and daredevil activities.

He liked to tell the story of leaving Italy. He came over by ship when he was in his twenties: the big voyage of his life, leaving a small mountain village in Italy, a village with no schools after grade three, where children like my dad were sent away to farms to pull a mule and cart. He left this village in search of a better life, a paying job.

"I sail for ten days! They take us to New York and we choose where to go. I go to Quebec."

The only time I witnessed Dad being gentle was in his garden, holding vegetables like they were newborn babies: zucchini, herbs, lettuce, onions, peppers, and rows and rows of tomatoes, his big fingers gently pulling the vegetables from the earth, from their roots and vines, transferring them to baskets lined with towels. Those hands that had the capacity to rip limbs and break necks also had the capacity for such sweetness, tenderness, but I would never have known it unless I witnessed his love for his garden. And sometimes when he saw me watching him, he would soften.

Maybe it was his own childhood brought to life, feeling like he was in the mountains of Italy, in the soil, digging through earth and leaves, producing such luscious fruits filled with colour and instant gratification. I liked to fantasize about Italy: I imagined it was warm and beautiful, like Sophia Loren. Dad always said the Italians made the best movies, but maybe it was just his mother tongue that made him feel at home.

"Joanna, come, come." He waved me over to where he stood in fresh soil. "Hold basket…. See, see the big tomato?" he said, holding up a large, ripe orange-red tomato, dimpled and round. "Take a bite, taste!"

I sank my mouth into the tomato, its juice dripping down my cheeks. He laughed and took a big bite, ate almost the whole thing, smiling, a magical moment I wished I could preserve like his tomato sauce and bottled wines in his cellar. But those moments were fractional, minutes out of years. His love for his garden was filled with warmth and wonder, but not for the vulnerability and expressions of his own children.

One day I ran into the garden with his shaving cream. I had fished it out of the medicine cabinet to create scientific experiments in the grass. I left the shaving cream outside, forgetting it until he stormed into the dining room and lifted me from my chair. He threw me into the kitchen, where I crashed into the fridge and fell to the ground. Then he kicked me with his steel-toed boots until he had no steam left in him and all the screams had been beaten out of me. I crawled on the floor like a slinking cat to get away and hid under my bed in the farthest unreachable corner, trembling. Lou found me. I saw Lou's curly red hair, her thick glasses pushing against her cheeks, and her big toothy grin as she lay on the ground to look under the bed.

Lou tucked her long hair behind her ear and began to sing. I eventually joined in until we got lost in music, making up songs. It helped me forget the panic.

"Gonna throw Papa into the sea when I'm big an' he can't see. Gonna throw Mama from a speeding train, oooo oooo oooo oooo."

Lou taught me to harmonize while we laughed and sang about killing our parents.

A few afternoons later, I was in the yard playing in the sprinkler. I ran inside to change, skipping past my mother's bedroom door on the way to mine. It was the middle of the day under a blazing sun, and Mother was lying down, moving around and breathing heavily, naked. She lifted the top sheet from her body when she saw me staring at her through the open door. She looked at me and caressed the side of the bed where my father usually slept, gestured for me. My heart was beating faster than normal, ahead of my mother's emptiness that tried to pull me in toward her bed like a magnet, as if she might swallow me whole and stop my heart from beating all together.

"Come lay down with Mommy. I'm lonely," she said.

"No, I don't want to lie down with you."

"I'm lonely," she said again and patted the empty side of the bed.

"No." I ran down the hall and out the door, letting it slam behind me, my heart pounding.

# CHAPTER FIVE

IT WAS 1976, and Montreal was hosting the Winter Olympics. People were arriving in the city by car, bus, train, and plane. Every night, newscasts reported on our athletes and the entertainment, and I was going to be part of it. I was almost chosen as the singer for the Olympic song, was the first runner-up, a source of severe disappointment for my mother. But I didn't care much, because I was dancing in the opening ceremony. That was good enough for me.

"How come you didn't dance when you were a girl?" I asked my mother, who clearly loved dance and *could* dance in spite of her 350 pounds. We were in her bedroom, talking about the Olympic show.

She turned away from me and stood in front of her dresser mirror, wearing a big white bra. Her breasts were propped up by her belly, which was round and popped out beyond her breasts. She wore underwear, and her pink dress covered in large green flowers was on the bed. She sprinkled baby powder all over her skin, rubbing it in.

"Because your grandmother wouldn't let me dance," she said.

"Why?"

"Because."

"Because why?"

She wouldn't answer at all and just ignored me. She had the blank look in her eyes, like I wasn't there. This was the mother that scared me most, the one with the dead eyes.

"Come here."

I walked toward her slowly, reluctantly. She put her arms around me to keep me there. I didn't want to be held or touched. I wanted to get out of the room, but she sat down at the edge of her bed and held me between her legs, rubbing me up and down my back. I was trapped. Above her bed was a painting of a ballerina on pointe, one leg up in the air, in a white tutu. I stared at her frozen in place above the bed and imagined being onstage with her, spinning, turning, and leaping into colours on the wall.

There were noises from outside. I could hear the other kids playing, running, and yelling. I pictured them in their homes with their families, playing board games or reading books. My mother was holding me hostage, squeezing me with her thighs. I understood there was something wrong with this and also that no one was going to rescue me.

Outside was where I felt most free, where birds and creatures crawled, hid, and flew. I wanted to be like them, to lift myself higher on the strength of my own muscles, to reach the sky and leave behind what was human.

When she let me go, I ran to my climbing tree in the yard, stood on its strong roots, and wrapped my arms around it as its bark caressed my cheek. The grooves reminded me of elephants with their deep wrinkles and curves. I felt love in the wild, soothed, as if the trees were like angels or gods. Maybe their branches were the arms of gods that cradled us when we climbed up into them to be held.

Climbing as high as my body could take me, I closed my eyes to see if I could balance on a thin branch. I felt alone, and in fact, I was. Sadie was gone, and no one spoke of her. I couldn't understand it, because I thought of her often. In my fort under the porch, I had special stones and toys that reminded me of her. I created a kind of altar to her. I missed her, and there was almost nothing left of her in our house, only an oil painting of her face from her confirmation, which hung in our living room like a photograph over a coffin.

I tried to avoid my dad as much as possible, and Diego was never home — always off playing football and being a teenager with his friends. As was Lou. They both drank, smoked pot, listened to Pink Floyd and Zeppelin, and tried to stay as far away from home as they could. When they were home, they huddled in the basement, getting high or pushing me out. Teenagers were their own breed, it seemed, and no one wanted an eight-year-old sibling around.

And Lou was starting to hate me.

Every time Mother spoke it was about me: about my dancing, my singing, my acting. "Joanne is dancing in the Olympic show."

Lou was justifiably resentful.

The jealousy between Lou and me grew into a living, breathing entity. She often screamed at me to "get the fuck away." Sometimes her threats turned into actions and I couldn't defend myself. I knew why: my mother loved me more than she loved Lou, she always had. I had figured out how to be what Mother wanted, how to please her, how to make her love me or what *I thought* was love: dancing, being close to her. *Yes, Mom. No, Mom. Thank you, Mom. I can do it, Mom. I'll be a star, Mother, if …*

When I auditioned for *Sesame Street*, I thought I'd hit the big time, though I was only eight years old. Make-believe was my great escape from reality. It was the only reality that I would come to love, the only true place where all of me could be present and free. I could back-talk, move, scream, laugh, and cry without any fear of violence. I could give full expression to my emotions.

Mother coached me on the way to the audition.

"And how do you present yourself when you greet the men who will hire you?"

"I say 'Hi, I'm Joanne, and it's a pleasure to meet you.'"

Mother fixed my shirt, then licked her fingers and smoothed my hair.

"Am I going to see Oscar, Ernie, and Bert?"

"I don't know. Remember, stand tall."

We walked through the doors, where a man with a beard and moustache met us. He ushered Mother to a chair in the lobby and gestured for her to sit.

Inside the booth were two men. It looked like the inside of a spaceship, with tall glass walls and buttons and speakers and film-strips in big round cans. I was in a studio with carpeted ceilings and floors and big leather couches. Headphones and large microphones hung above me or stood in stands, and there was a screen that seemed as big as a movie-theatre screen. A large image of Big Bird and Oscar appeared before my eyes. I had only ever seen them on a small televi-sion set. This truly was magic. If Mother's dream for me included Big Bird, recording studios, stages, and Olympic ceremonies, I would gladly make the magical world my dream, too. And I did. I was hired and would be working for *Sesame Street*. My first booked gig.

A few days after the audition, I was getting ready for school and walked by the washroom. Mother sat on the toilet with the door open, naked. I stopped. She didn't close the door, which was in easy reach from the seat. She didn't say anything, just stared at me. There was no toilet paper so she grabbed a towel that hung from the rack, wiped herself with it, and widened her legs with her woman parts exposed, her eyes empty, like a dead person.

After running out of the house with my shoes in my hand, I stopped at the end of the block where I was supposed to wait for the yellow bus to take me to my grade-two class. Instead, I started to walk.

I pulled my socks off and put them in my bag with my shoes and walked along the concrete barefoot. It was a hot morning, and the road and sidewalks were spotted with sticky soda, wads of gum, little tuffs of grass poking through the cracks, discarded cigarette butts, and broken glass. The concrete was warm beneath my feet.

My mother always said things like "Don't touch the stove burners" and "Look before you cross the road." I didn't understand how getting burned or touching the edge of a sharp knife could hurt more than being kicked on my bare-skinned legs by my father.

I continued to walk along the path to school and came across a pile of broken green glass.

I stared at the bottle in shards below me and decided to walk through it, gently, as if walking on thin ice, my arms outstretched like I was on a gymnast's beam, glass slicing into the skin under my feet. I walked on, making bloody footprints all the way to school.

# CHAPTER SIX

MY PARENTS FINALLY divorced, and child abuse was cited as the reason.

Living without my father was the greatest blessing. The routine of shows and performances dominated my days. There wasn't a weeknight that wasn't filled with dance or theatre, and I was just learning to relax at home, without the threat of violence, when the unthinkable happened — again. He came back.

First it was for one weekend, and then another, then another, until he was with us every weekend. He wasn't supposed to be near us according to the social services and divorce agreement. I had been secure in my new freedom and was utterly devastated and confused by his "weekend" visits. He would come and go and stayed in my mother's bedroom at night, and it would be theirs again as if he hadn't left. He assumed his previous role, barking orders, expecting breakfast and clean clothes, and expecting his "family" to respond to his commands during his two-day sleepovers.

He stood over me one Sunday morning while I vacuumed and repeatedly hit me whenever I missed a spot. Then, on one of his weekend visits, I decided to rebel. I knew that he wasn't supposed to be there, that this was a violation of the court's order that Mother seemed fine with. It was morning, and I was expected to stay inside to sweep the furnace room and garage. I refused, screaming, "I don't have to listen to you anymore and you are not allowed to hit me or you're in big trouble!"

He muttered something with his backhand up, then walked away from me. I was only nine, but had stood up to this hulking man who towered above me. It had taken a while to find my voice that day. After sitting with the broomstick in the damp, dark space of the furnace room for what felt like an eternity, I decided I would not clean. I practised what I might say over and over in my head. And when he returned to see that I hadn't swept, he tried to threaten me, but then I found it: courage. He never tried to hit me ever again, and he knew he did not own me anymore, or maybe I finally understood that fact. But it was over.

What hadn't ended were his weekend sleepovers. He could not let go of what he thought was his, his right to exert power over the girls and woman he spent time with. But it was more than that. I heard them making noise behind the closed bedroom door. One afternoon, I tried to make myself scarce when they emerged. I stayed inside the house, watched cartoons in the basement. I heard Mother holler, "We're going to go grocery shopping and to the hardware store. You be good!" It meant there would be enough time to rummage in that bedroom.

I'm not certain why I believed I would find a clue to the strange weekend sleepovers I despised, or why my mother thought it was acceptable after the court case and the drama of exposing physical abuse. It made no sense that she, a woman who had packed up a car to escape with her children, had taken him back and then gone through an actual divorce years later only to repeat the pattern of letting him back in on weekends. But it wasn't about safety, protecting us from violence. The courts said he needed to be removed and that he was not to come to our home, that we were to visit with him outside of the home. Breaking the rules didn't matter.

I went to her bedroom, the painted ballerina on the wall my only witness. I opened the closets and searched through the bedside table. I opened a wooden drawer at the bottom of a wardrobe unit to find a few dozen books and magazines hidden away. There were images of naked grown-ups and little blue reading books. When I opened them and tried to read some of the passages, words like *cock* stood out. It was her secret drawer. I muttered to myself in disgust and let the blue books drop back into their hiding place like garbage.

I told Lou about my findings, tried to usher her into the room when Mother wasn't there. She helped put the pieces of the puzzle together: that they were having sex behind those doors at night, and in the morning, or whenever the doors were closed.

The scenario of the abused wife with children was real, only my mother was more interested in satisfying her own desires than in protecting her children. This wasn't new. It was just more overt. Only, she never said a word in explanation, which left me constantly attempting to reorder reality so I could find solid ground. I couldn't.

It was hard to make sense out of abusive parents. Wasted time.

One night we were silently eating dinner with him at our table. He lifted his backhand to demonstrate that he was going to hit our mother. He didn't, but Lou and I looked at each other and I screamed, not out of fear, but out of rage. I grabbed my fork and knife, one in each hand, banged them on the table beside my plate, and just howled like an animal. Oddly, nothing happened. My father smirked as if it were a joke. Lou stared, and my mother ignored me for a while until she finally screamed, "That's enough!"

I stood and left the table. After that weekend, the sex visits ceased, and Dad never came back.

Lou and I visited him in his basement apartment, but it was a forced visitation. He wanted to see us, though I don't know why. At first we saw him on holidays or for family events, but by the time I turned ten, he would disappear. Years later, when we resumed minimal contact, he said Mother kept us from him. Maybe she did, maybe she didn't. I don't know, and I simply didn't care.

No one asked what I wanted, ever. If he had asked, I would have told him that I didn't want to see him and I didn't want to live with my mother, but no one ever asked me anything. I knew that both my parents were disturbed; I just didn't know how to speak that truth. Or who to speak it to.

# CHAPTER SEVEN

WE MOVED AGAIN when I was eleven. I left some of my toys and the altar to Sadie under the porch.

We moved from a suburb of Montreal to NDG, or Notre-Dame-de-Grâce, an area with a large Italian and European immigrant population mixed in with some local French-Canadian homeowners. We rented an apartment in a house, only this time it was just my mother, Lou, and I. Diego had already left for college. The move happened in the middle of sixth grade for me, and now I was the new girl. My social life was non-existent in this place where some very hard-core Italian eleven-year-olds owned the hallways and the yard. I didn't want to mess with them.

I didn't fit in, and my mother didn't help. She sent me to school with rollers in my hair for auditions or recitals. I hid in lockers and tried to convince myself that I would be a star, that the other children were unimportant and this was the sacrifice for this unknown thing called fame. I had Big Bird and studios. I had the stage. That's what this was for.

But I would say no to the rollers after a particularly gruelling bullying session with the mean girl, Maria.

"I'll see you in the courtyard after school," she said one day during lunch.

I tried to run home when school was out, but the entire sixth grade encircled me. Then Maria joined me in the middle. I held my books and tried to exit the circle, but it was meant to be some sort of ritual, of children following the orders of the loudest, of the leader. "Roller-face. Idiot. Fight. Fight. Fight." It was all I heard, the chanting. My books were pushed out of my arms and Maria's fists went up.

"Fight! Fight! Fight!" everyone screamed.

Then a lone boy broke the chain, hollering, "Leave her alone. Run!"

It seemed a brave act for one child in the face of the mob, but it worked. His defence of me broke the curse that day. After that, I tried to remain as invisible as possible.

But then there was my mother.

I was embarrassed by her, by her 350 pounds, shameful of me as that was. People gawked at her as if she had a disease or were lazy. She was neither lazy nor diseased, just damaged, and her layers of body weight were the result.

Mother always heard the classic phrases that large women were told, like "You have such a beautiful *face*." She was never consoled by these backhanded compliments. They were hurtful. To her and to me.

When children called her horrible things like "fat ass," or when they would ask if she had eaten a house, I would scream back "Shut up!" or "Mind your own business!" Sometimes Mother and I would just pretend we didn't hear anything. But I didn't want her to drive me to school. It was hard enough making friends and I didn't want to give the children additional ammunition to make fun of or bully me.

But separating from my mother was like skinning an animal. One day, when she drove me to school, I asked her to drop me off a block away from the building. She stopped, turned the engine off, looked right into my eyes with such vulnerability and asked, "Is it because I'm fat?"

It was.

"No, it's not that…. I just don't want them to think I'm a baby. Don't want to be dropped off by my mother. I want to seem more grown-up."

She never drove me again. I walked every day after that exchange and felt enormous guilt. I tried to cover, protect her feelings, but I'm not so sure she believed me. I would never do it again either, ask her to hide or not be seen; well, actually, I would ask her to go away many times as I got older, but it had nothing to do with her body size.

My mother's two escapes were food and me — specifically, my growing career. I had been taking acting-for-camera lessons, and she was submitting me for television and film auditions as my "manager." My first movie was called *Hard Feelings*, directed by Daryl Duke, when I was eleven going on twelve. I flew to Atlanta and North Carolina, was put up in hotels, and had a taste of what an actor's life could be like away from my hometown.

The movie was set in the sixties, with props and clothing of the era. It was like a human version of a dollhouse, with life-sized furniture that would be swapped out depending on the scene: dining tables in place of living room couches, walls that went down and up, and interior worlds that came to life with all of us actors placed on our marks inside our make-believe house. Large cameras with rolls of 35 mm film, massive set lights, microphones, and crew — makeup, hair, wardrobe — were scattered everywhere.

We did take after take of scenes in close-up, medium, and wide shots. It was magic, like *The Wizard of Oz* come to life. I bought yellow pants and my first cowboy hat with my per diem, which was the only pay I would see, because the cheques were made out to my manager, not to me. The union had yet to protect children in the seventies and eighties.

I wore those yellow pants with pride, along with my "Kiss me, I'm Italian" T-shirt, until Mother said, "You need to work on wearing smaller pant sizes." She had noticed my yellow pants were getting a little tight and told me I was getting big. I didn't want her sizing me up. It took so little to humiliate me at that age (at any age), and if wearing my favourite yellow pants inspired negative commentary or her horrible gaze, then those yellow pants were better off left folded and hidden in my dresser drawer for good.

"You're getting fat," my mother said another day, more directly, leaning over the couch where I was listening to Queen on the record player.

I entered the music, raged as loud as the hard rock that bounced off the walls from the speakers. She was base. She was beneath the lowest sound I could make, an unreachable mother whose body was four times the size of mine. She was like the entire wild pack of sixth-graders circling me. I was determined to ascend somehow, to lift out and away from her clutches and her objectification of my body. Perhaps she was blurting out her innermost fears or hatred about fat. It would backfire.

"Get away from me." I swatted her with my hand while my body seized and stiffened on the couch. If I could have punched her I would have, but I shunned her instead.

She stood up, wounded like a shot deer, and limped away to her bedroom.

# CHAPTER EIGHT

MARTHA WAS MY drama teacher and had been for five years. She was adored by the adults and students alike. She wasn't shy, and no discussions were off-limits. Martha had no kid filter. Conversations included theatre, productions, the Beatles, war, penises, breasts and vaginas, and sex and more sex. She was everything my mother was not. She wore scarves and turtlenecks with skirts, leg warmers, and sneakers; she had long, thick black hair and shiny eyes like buffed obsidian stones; and she chain-smoked her Rothmans cigarettes. Martha was magnetic, and I was drawn to her. Mother was, too, always extending dinner invitations or offering to make costumes for all the students. Martha founded her own theatre company.

I was twelve years old when our family moved again, and I was in the car with Martha when we pulled into the lot outside our new building: a high-rise on a bus strip with a concrete underpass beneath the train tracks. Moving schools and apartments was becoming a habit.

I was going to be auditioning for Juilliard, and Martha would be my coach. The two of us sat at the kitchen table with my mother, talking about New York, monologue choices, and photo sessions.

This was the beginning of the triangle between Martha, Mother, and me. I didn't know anything about Juilliard, but the idea of going to New York was exciting.

The following morning I was barely awake, sitting at the table with my Wheaties sprinkled with sugar, when Mother entered to make an announcement. "I've arranged for you to have image-consultant lessons with Sylvia."

I had no idea what she was talking about. I was twelve, barely knew I had an image, or who I was even, but the increasingly magnified attention on my body was becoming emotionally dangerous. I screamed that I would not have my image consulted with anyone, but she carried on.

"Oh yes, you are, young lady, and she's on her way." My mother pointed at me, then poured herself a Coca-Cola while I ate.

"Now?"

"Yes, now."

"But why didn't you ask me?"

"Because you would have argued like you're doing now."

I stared at her with defiance. *Whatcha gonna do about it? You can't make me do this image stuff, what!* "What?"

"Don't you 'what' me, young lady, or I'll get your father to come over here to deal with you."

"Fuck you, Helen." She hated that I had started to call her by her first name, let alone that I had started swearing at her.

"Do you think you can talk to me like that and get away with it?" Mother was agitated, shaking.

"I'll talk to you how I like."

"You watch your mouth." Her voice broke and she turned away from me, digging dishes out of the drying rack, clinking and cracking, her fingers clenched around ceramic, reaching up to put them in cupboards while her hands shook.

"And if someone needs their image consulted, it's you." I stared at her without flinching.

"Why don't you care about me?" she asked.

"No one cares about you."

I had crossed the line, but it was too late, I couldn't take the words back. The doorbell rang. Mother wiped her teary eyes without saying a word.

It was the image consultant, Sylvia. She was round and she wore baggy black clothes. She dropped some books on the table; one of them was titled *The History of Costumes*.

It was a long hour.

"Did you know that the perfect size for a woman is thirty-six for the bust, twenty-six for the waist, and thirty-five inches for the hips?"

She told me she would measure and weigh me every week as part of our "lessons." The goal was to work toward the ideal size of a woman. She pulled out the yellow measuring tape that first day, while my half-eaten cereal sat on the table in front of me. She chattered on about how eating cereal was okay but sprinkling sugar on top was not, and on and on until she wrapped the tape around my rigid body to evaluate my imperfections. I sucked in my waist before she said "twenty-eight inches."

It confirmed how fat I was — two inches bigger than the perfect female size. I held in my breath and looked down to hide my quivering lip.

The following week I locked myself in the bathroom as the hour passed. Sylvia got paid to sit at the kitchen table in silence, but I didn't get measured. I lay in the tub fully dressed while Sylvia knocked on the door. She eventually left.

I called myself names inside my head — *ugly* and *fat* — desperately wanting to get rid of something inside myself, be rid of everything inside me; not just food, but the memories of childhood, of sisters screaming or the mewl of helpless kittens being bludgeoned to death, of my mother's obsession with me. I shook and couldn't catch my breath, wasn't able to control my body or mind. I dropped to the floor and rocked back and forth, overwhelmed by fear, and in that instant I was back in the kitchen where my father was pulling me off the kitchen floor by my hair with his large hands and kicking my bare skin with his Kodiak boots. I didn't know that I was twelve and not eight, didn't know that I was on the floor of my bathroom and not on the kitchen floor being beaten.

Flashbacks. They were new to me. Before the age of twelve, I hadn't experienced flashbacks, and I had no idea what they were. I believed I was going crazy. After regaining control of my breath and opening my eyes, I remembered where I was. My limbs were numb; my head and face felt disconnected from my spine. I shook my legs to regain feeling and finally stood up, aware of my surroundings.

I paced in the washroom, wanted to scratch my skin. I did. Scratched and scratched until deep red marks appeared on my arms. I opened the medicine cabinet and found a razor, grabbed it, and thinly sliced across my wrist, producing a tiny red mark. I focused on it, sat on top of the toilet seat in a type of haze, and was calm again.

My image-consulting lessons with Sylvia abruptly ended.

But Martha stepped in. She helped my mother groom me for stardom. She prepped me for Juilliard and New York. My CV and headshots were set up, with photographs of multiple looks: they clicked and snapped me in my *Vogue* winter look in a woollen hat. *Click.* And the terrified girl with tears in her eyes. *Click.* The tough-girl shot with the hard face. *Click.* And the feminine look, complete with lace-frilled top, curled hair, and makeup. *Click. Click. Click.*

Meanwhile, Mother arranged auditions for television shows and theatre productions: at Saidye Bronfman, the Centaur, CBC. She told everyone she was my manager. I envisioned her as a caricature of a white male producer with a cigar hanging out of her mouth, round glasses, and a moustache: *Oh yes, my daughter started professionally on* Sesame Street. *Joanne is in a new TV show for teen-agers.* Or, *I turned down the* Mickey Mouse Club *when they were scouting. She was only five at the time, didn't want her to move away from home.* Then an independent filmmaker asked if I could do a nude scene at the age of twelve. After seriously considering it, Mother, thankfully, said no. Thankfully.

I had friends now, too. Steffin, Georgia, and Patrick were in Martha's company. Steffin was seventeen, fat, gay, and sarcastic, with long dirty-blond hair. Georgia was twelve, had light-brown skin, and wore a black miniskirt with fishnets. I would sneak peeks at her when she wasn't looking; something about her made me breathe a little faster than usual. Patrick was also gay, with long brown hair dyed jet-black and a faux-fur scarf. He dressed like a girl and used Nerf balls he had cut in half for breasts. He lived in foster care and called himself Splash. He changed his name as often as he changed homes, and that was often.

The four of us were rehearsing our original stage play in the large main space of our studio in Saint-Henri. We were the leads. Martha was shouting stage directions at us all when a boy I hadn't seen before entered the studio. He had thick blond hair and beautiful green eyes. He wore dirty faded jeans and a T-shirt, with a pack of smokes sitting on his shoulder under his shirt like a shoulder pad and a cigarette lodged above his ear. His name was Clint.

Steffin and Splash salivated over his Marlboro Man good looks, trying to outdo each other without speaking as they stretched, coughed, and waved their hands. If gay was visible, it was hard to miss those two. Georgia couldn't have cared less. She bit her nails, then looked at her fingers. I tried to seem uninterested, but I couldn't help but stare at Clint.

He was the male version of Georgia, but older, and was as overtly masculine as she was feminine, and just as hypnotic. I had been on a few dates up to that point, had kissed a few boys. The only girl who made me feel like kissing her was Georgia, but I shied away and didn't know if what I was experiencing was real, or if she would want me to. Being with a girl seemed taboo, too intimate, terrifying, and I didn't dare give it much conscious thought. Clint was a boy many girls seemed attracted to, as well as adult women, even Martha, who sexualized everyone, young or not. She had a thirty-five-year-old friend named Bev who used to tell me she thought Clint was attractive. She used to drive him around, and many years later Clint told me Bev gave him a blowjob in the front seat of her car.

My friends and I headed to Mount Royal after rehearsal to do what teenagers like us did: drink, do drugs, make out. We made our own curfews, defied the rules of our guardians or parents. We were the raw ones, or the queer ones, and we were incredibly stubborn. We made fun how and when we wanted.

I invited Clint to come with us, and though he seemed resistant because of my age (he thought I was too young), he came anyway. He kept calling me "kid," which annoyed me and yet inspired me to pursue him. It was dark out when we climbed the mountain, the cross shining brightly above us in the warm air. Steffin was flirting with Clint, which he did with all the boys.

"Come on, what you so afraid of? Think I'm going to do something to you?" Steffin struck a flamboyant pose. We all laughed except for Clint.

"Lighten up. You can't catch being gay." I was the last person to give advice on lightening up. I was the girl who drew ink drawings of coffins with dead flowers around them and earned the nickname Black-Monday. But I was intent on kissing this boy, and I did. We didn't stop kissing until I heard laughter coming from behind the bushes. I smiled at Clint and took off at a run toward Georgia, Splash, and Steffin.

Meanwhile, I was in the final phase of my rehearsals for Julliard, a solo performance of my monologues: *Romeo and Juliet*,

*Medea*, and a contemporary piece. Martha and I worked weekly, and the studio was converted into a theatre, filled with about fifty chairs, tables, hors d'oeuvres, and wine for the audience.

At the end of my last monologue, I heard the applause and bowed while people yelled "Bravo!" Clint sat behind my mother, clapping. We smiled at each other, and Mother turned to look at him, then back at me. I looked away from her.

Adults were getting drunk, Tom Waits blared through the speakers, and my one-woman show turned into a party. Even my mother wiggled about in her best dress, made of floral-patterned velvet, while she nibbled on cucumber and cream cheese sandwiches, accepting praise for my talents like a proud peacock.

Georgia, Splash, Steffin, and I snuck into a washroom stall and drank red wine from plastic cups. Splash pulled out a spliff and we lit up.

"Kiss me, Splash." Steff touched Splash's thigh.

"Oh please, Miss Thing," Splash said, "you don't have enough money."

Georgia giggled, sitting on my lap, cupping my neck with her hands for balance. I tried to ignore the shivers I felt while my friend cradled my legs. I was incredibly attracted to her, but I was dating Clint and not quite aware of what was going on with my body.

"What are you kids doing in there?" It was my mother.

"Is that marijuana?" asked another woman from behind the door.

We heard taps turning on while Splash and Steffin laughed. "We're busy, Mrs. V."

"Is Joanne in there?"

Georgia put her hand over my mouth and Steffin responded no.

"She's not with Clint, is she?"

How did she even know his name?

"Seriously, Steff ... will you take some advice from me if I give it to you?" my mother asked.

"Uhhh, no," he replied.

The boys laughed. We were rude.

"I can't believe your mouth, young man, and for goodness' sake, next time use the boy's washroom, will you?"

Georgia and I suppressed our giggles. She whispered in my ear before my mother left the bathroom. Her lips so close sent another shiver up my spine. I tried to pretend I felt nothing, even though every part of me wanted to kiss her.

# CHAPTER NINE

NEW YORK. It felt like home with its tall buildings, lights, yellow cabs, theatres, corner carts, trolleys, horses, and Central Park. Men and women stood on every street corner with pretzel and hotdog carts. There were stores with cigarette packs lining walls, key chains with apples, portable stereos, beat boxes with speakers of every size, watches, calculators, and gadgets, and restaurants everywhere. Electric.

It was fall, and the winds were so strong they blew Lou right off the sidewalk, which was the start of her disdain for the entire trip. We ate at the popular Leo Lindy's, a deli where black-and-white photographs and signatures of stars lined the walls. The menu included the Carol Burnett side dish, the Jack Benny egg dish, and the Lucille Ball special platter. We saw the Rockettes perform at Radio City Music Hall, *Agnes of God* off-Broadway with Amanda Plummer (whom I worked with many years later), and *A Chorus Line* on Broadway. I loved every second of it.

This was the city that held my childhood fantasies right in reach. The possibility of becoming a professional actor felt real.

Juilliard.

I had to audition three times after an 8:00 a.m. check-in. Hundreds of us lined the hallways of the school, speaking to ourselves, stretching, clearing our throats from morning until night. We were ushered into a large room and asked to choose an animal, become the animal, then take a bath as the animal. I was a cat, meowing and scratching away at the side of the tub, finding a way to leap out, stretching on an imaginary blanket to purr, occasionally licking my front paw. I watched all the other hopefuls wildly behaving like animals all around me and took in all the older auditioning actors while adults walked around us with their clipboards and pens, marking sheets.

We all waited as time slowly passed and we continued to prepare for the first round of auditions. Some were visibly nervous, sweating as they read out loud from their monologues scribbled on paper, or listening to beat boxes with headsets, practising in whispers in corners and stairways everywhere. I was taking in my competitors, who felt like kindred spirits. All our dreams hung in the air, and we would have to crush each other to achieve them. Hundreds of us would be cut down to forty for the second round, where we would have to audition again, and then, after six hours of auditions and cuts, we would be cut down to five hopefuls. A notice would go up on a corkboard each time, until we were down to the last short list.

When I looked up at the list tacked to the board, I saw the typed font with my name, Joanne Vannicola, second from the top. There had been so many disappointed faces leaving the building all day, but here I was in the top five, so close it could be real; this life, this city, could maybe be my home. I wanted it, let myself believe I could live there. Prior to this I had been mostly going through the motions, not really thinking ahead, just getting through the days.

I had an interview with four adults who were seated behind a large table in a room with ceiling-high windows. I sat in the middle of the mostly empty room, facing the table.

"You're only thirteen years old."

"Yes."

"We've never had anyone your age in the theatre department in our program. We've had the occasional musician, but the theatre department here is different than the musical department," one of the men said. He had a moustache, a beard, and a soothing voice. "It's emotionally intensive. How would you feel about leaving home at the age of thirteen?" he asked.

"Don't know, good. I would feel good," I said nervously, but didn't know how to answer the questions. My mouth was dry as I shyly started to answer with one-word responses.

"Do you know the city?"

"No."

"Do you know anyone in New York?"

"No."

"Have you ever been away from home?"

I stumbled over my words. "You mean on purpose?"

"Pardon me?" asked a beautiful woman sitting beside the man — the kind of beautiful woman I had seen in movie pictures, with long coiffed hair and makeup and wearing an expensive-looking dress with matching gloves and handbag.

"What do you mean 'on purpose'?"

I jiggled my legs up and down in the chair and rattled, "'Cause a kid could be away from home if they ran away, or they could be away from home if someone was keeping them for a while if they fought with their mother all the time or social services paid a visit, or they could be in a foster home like my friend Patrick. Well, he changed his name to Splash, and anyway, his parents didn't want him and his mother is crazy. Or I guess they could go to a place like Juilliard and that could be on purpose, right?"

The room fell silent. Four faces looked back at me, paper and pens poised in front of them. I was not prepared to speak unscripted. I had only worked on the monologues and was confident in the characters and my ability to inhabit them, but I could not hold a conversation or find the language to express my thoughts. I was afraid I had blown it. My legs shook up and down and my foot hit the floor over and over, *tap, tap, tap.*

*Don't sniffle or rub your nose or slouch,* I said to myself, squirming in the chair and adjusting my body. Two of the adults looked at each other before the man spoke. "I think we're done. I want you to know something, Joanne. You were very, very good. If we don't accept you this year, we want you to come back when you are older, okay?"

"Okay."

They would be accepting only three out of the five of us. Mother and I looked at the last sheet and my name wasn't on it. I turned to look back down the hall as we walked toward the exit, and the beautiful woman was staring back at me. She smiled and waved. I waved back. I wanted to be with her and start a new life, to walk the hallways for years. I hadn't realized how much I wanted it until it was over; I hadn't given it much thought, what living in New York could be like. I tried to cover my disappointment and faced my mother as if it didn't matter. Her disappointment was visible enough for the two of us, even if she didn't speak.

I replayed in my head the Juilliard meeting after three rounds of exhaustive auditions, wondered what I could have done to change their minds. I hadn't been prepared for conversation, only for rehearsed dialogue, but if I could have said anything, if I had only been prepared, I would have told them, "I *must* leave. I *must* be in this school. I am more ready than all the twenty-year-olds and I need it more. I don't care if I don't have family or friends in New York, just accept me." It could have changed my life, the course, could have changed what was to come for the next few years. If only. The real dialogue would have been "I need out, I need to get away from my mother, from the suffocating pressure, and New York might save me."

If only the young were taught to communicate with adults. Maybe some were, but no one I knew.

Mother was gloomy and Lou was unbearable. She swore and muttered to herself the whole walk away from Juilliard.

"Can't you be happy for your sister? Don't you want to have fun?" Mother said. It was another cold day in New York.

Lou shouted back, "Why don't you leave me alone!" Her back rounded as she stared down a city drain like it might catch the tears she hid from our mother. Lou hated being with us in New York. She was the tagalong; I knew it but tried not to give it attention.

An appointment was set up for me with an A-list talent agency that represented models and actresses. Mother and Lou were outside in the waiting room while I sat across from a man in front of a large wooden desk covered with papers and photographs. He stared at me for a while, then looked at my photos and resumé while I nervously waited for him to talk to me. He looked up at me for a few beats, and then waved his hand in the air, gesturing for me to move. "Stand up."

I stood up and he continued to stare.

"Turn around slowly," he said.

I felt naked, exposed. I dared not speak back or say no. I was not trained for no, and men in positions of power seemed to know they held the strings.

I turned slowly, faced him, and waited for him to speak.

"Lose five pounds and come back again to see me." He stared at me without uttering another word.

I ran out of his office and past my mother and Lou, who were submerged in cushy leather-upholstered chairs, reading magazines. I ran until I was outside.

They both tried to keep up with me, my mother asking what had happened. I couldn't tell her how he'd undressed me with his eyes *like she did*. Everything reduced to five pounds of body weight and flesh.

*Too young.*

*Five pounds too fat.*

I believed I was ready, had made it to the top five in auditions at Juilliard. I wanted it. But after all those months of preparation, it was over.

I wouldn't be moving to New York.

# CHAPTER TEN

AFTER NEW YORK, Lou and I rarely spoke to each other. Lou had taken to reading tarot cards and smoking quite a bit of weed. Our room turned into a mini-shrine with candles, rocks, beads, and knick-knacks. We had little in common other than the hatred of our mother, a love for music, and old wounds, but she was still my big sister and could take me down. Normally we argued, so it was odd when she did speak up for me.

"I have beer, you guys. Please stay. Don't leave," Mother said to Clint and me, begging us not to leave her alone.

"Get out, you guys. You don't have to stay with her," Lou said.

Mother's hands were curled into fists. "Joanne, Clint. Stay!"

Lou defended us, telling our mother that we were not her babysitter, but the fight escalated until our mother snapped.

"You mind your business, you little bitch." Mother grabbed Lou by the hair at the back of her head and repeatedly called her a bitch.

Clint and I escaped the fight and ran under the bridge on Cavendish Boulevard. We avoided talking about what had happened, only throwing out one-word encapsulations while we ran:

*nuts, fucked, freaks.* We ended up at the Rose Bowl bowling alley at the end of the block, where we played Space Invaders and pinball, and smoked cigarettes.

A small group of men in blue shirts and dress pants were bowling, and while pins crashed and fell, Clint and I wandered away for privacy.

"I'm just going to kiss you right here," he said, kissing my neck and lips and touching me over my shirt. He gently asked, "Is this okay?"

I nodded yes and looked to see that we were still alone, then I practised touching him over his jeans. We kissed endlessly, staying out as late as we felt like. I wanted Clint to be as far away from my family as possible. But it was dark and we decided to make our way back to the apartment. We stole one last kiss before going in together.

"Finally, you're home. I've been waiting for you," Mother said. She was seated at the table in her white nightgown.

"Waiting for what?" I asked. "Where's Lou?"

"Out." Mother looked at me and changed the subject. "I bought a case of beer." She stood up and went into the kitchen.

Entering our apartment was like squeezing inside clothing too small, everything tight and uncomfortable. My mother sat down with two beers, one for herself and one for Clint. I went to get a beer from the fridge.

"Hey, hey, not for you," she said.

"Why can't I have a beer?"

"You're too young."

"I am not too young. What am I gonna do, maybe get a bit drunk and fall asleep in my own bed? Wow." I paused. "But you're giving Clint beer."

"Clint is almost sixteen. He's old enough to have a few beers," she said, patronizing me.

The new triangle was forming.

It wasn't routine behaviour for a parent to buy alcohol for a teenager, but my mother knew he liked to drink. She treated him like a contemporary, a friend. She was slick, could charm my friends with food or alcohol all she wanted, but I knew the real Helen. Lou had warned me. She once called our mother a black hole. How were we to deal with a parent that gave our friends the things they desired? It made her cool, fun. Everyone liked Mrs. V., until they crossed her. Even Lou would not escape her wrath that night, but Clint sat obliviously drinking his beer while hers sat untouched on the table. She didn't like beer. I didn't want to look at her. I went to my room and went to bed, but Clint stayed at the table, wanting to drink.

I woke up to a fight, opened my bedroom door and peered around the corner. Lou and my mother were arguing. I heard my mother say, "You're a bad influence on Joanne," and more, until she screamed, "You have to leave, Lou. I'll be damned if I let you stay here. I'm not stupid. You don't think I can teach you a thing or two, why, you got a big surprise coming."

"I know why you are doing this —"

Mother interrupted. "You shut the fuck up, Lou, you hear me?"

"I know what you are up to, buying beer and keeping them home —"

"Shut up!" My mother screamed so loudly I jumped out in full view.

They stared at me and everything went quiet. I didn't want Lou to leave, couldn't understand why she was being ejected from our home. She hadn't done anything that was worth being displaced.

"Where am I supposed to go? I'm only eighteen."

My mother told her to find an apartment, reiterating that she was a bad influence on me, which was a lie. Lou and I barely spent any time together, and all the "bad" behaviours I exhibited were a result of my actions, not Lou's. But once again my mother had a way of creating a reality that didn't exist, pitting child against child, tossing Lou out because of me — or so she said. I didn't want to be responsible, but that was the script, or what I felt internally.

"Take it back," I said to my mother.

"I'm going." Lou cut me off.

I couldn't see beyond my own culpability and I wanted to fix it, but my mother sat defiantly as if she had been hard done by. Always the fucking victim.

I followed Lou to our bedroom while she packed a bag, but we didn't speak. She crammed a skirt, a bra, a shirt, and other belongings into her luggage. I found a crumpled red two-dollar bill and gave it to her. Lou pushed the money into her purse as we stared at each other awkwardly.

"Lou … don't go," I said as I followed her out of our room to the front door. I tried to stop her, but she didn't have a choice. Mother sat at the table, resolute. Lou looked at me before opening the door as if she wanted to tell me something, but instead she turned and walked away without another word.

I left my mother at the table, slammed my bedroom door, and sat on my bed. I opened a wind-up ballerina jewellery box and pulled out a small tinfoil packet, unravelled it until I found the white papery acid, and put it under my tongue.

Every other family member had slowly been removed. The only one who had made it out normally — off to university — was Diego. He was the only one who could do no wrong in our house.

It wasn't his fault he was the only boy. It may have been a blessing for him in our family, but he learned horrible lessons about gender, too. My father once told him that if we girls got out of hand while our parents were out, he should beat us. Diego followed those orders, and once he beat Lou up with a broomstick. I watched it all, hiding around corners, behind furniture, listening, learning everything there was to know about men and women, girls and boys, our worth. But Diego didn't get hugged or read to at bedtime, either. He was expected to be a man, not cry, be strong. If he ever cried, he got shit.

I wished that Diego could have stopped my mother from throwing Lou out. Sometimes she listened to him, our surrogate father. He sat with her during "family" discussions, scolding the girls over something, her partner in crime. Consequently, he became hated by his siblings and respected by his parents. He was the capable one, the good child, the man.

When the acid kicked in, I could forget about my siblings, forget about Lou's departure. I went on a child's acid trip, stepped inside Barbie's trailer with her for tea and ended up in an amusement park on a Ferris wheel with the crowds below me.

I heard a voice inside myself speaking to me, and I responded until I decided the voice wasn't real. When I checked my watch, it was four in the morning. I went to the fridge and pulled out a single carrot. I peeled the carrot down to the size of a baby finger and put it in my mouth. I lit a match, trying to light the carrot stick until I realized it was a vegetable and not a cigarette at all. I tiptoed to my bedroom and fell onto my bed laughing. The white walls were breathing, moving in and out.

I stuck my head out the window to get away from the moving walls. I stared at a tree, but it was breathing too. Everything was breathing in and out — the night sky, the leaves, parked cars, even the moon. Why hadn't I seen the moon breathe before? I held myself and rocked back and forth to the rhythm of breath all around me. I looked at the moon again and wondered if it were possible for the moon and sun to collide, to explode and scatter fallen ashes around the Earth like dust.

# CHAPTER ELEVEN

MARTHA'S POLITICAL children's theatre company was a hit in Montreal. We brought attention to the issues of our generation. We talked and wrote plays about parents, education, race relations, choice, and gay rights. This was unique in the 1970s and 1980s, giving voice to race and gender issues. We carried signs about social justice issues up and down the streets — "Children's rights are human rights" — and sang "Give Peace a Chance." Reporters and other members of the press reviewed our shows. Newspaper clippings piled up. The famous cartoonist Aislin even did a cartoon about our theatre company.

We younger kids talked politics and sex with the older ones. They were far more knowledgeable, and I tried to pay attention as they bantered about HIV and AIDS. One kid called it a gay disease, a plague.

Clint and I discussed sex all the time. We were in love and it was mostly innocent, exploratory. But that innocence fell away one day.

"Your mother asked me what you and I do together sexually," Clint said. "She told me I was too old for you, that kissing was okay, but nothing more."

"Seriously? *Seriously!*"

It felt like another deep violation: My mother inserting herself into my first relationship, asking questions about what we did sexually, crossing new boundaries, and manipulating my boyfriend. It felt like she was taking more away from me. Nothing was sacred, private, not even sexual exploration as a teen with another teen. It was the beginning of the wedge between Clint and me.

The only person I trusted was Steffin. Somehow, he seemed to know everything, could see the storms before they arrived. But he was only a boy — well, hardly a boy. His life changed after his mother died. He had to fend for himself in ways children shouldn't, for shelter, safety, money. But it wasn't our queerness alone that connected us (I was still in the closet and would think about girls only on rare occasions, then deeply bury those thoughts); like so many damaged kids, we gravitated toward each other and toward darkness.

Steffin and I met up on Saint Catherine Street one afternoon before rehearsal, outside an old pub with darkened windows. It was a small place that older men frequented. The midafternoon sun was bright and the bar was filled with local drunks and businessmen in suits stealing away for drinks and more; the family men, Steffin called them, the ones with wives, who sought out sex with boys.

"I'm going to hide under the table and suck the dick of that guy in there. Don't get caught staring at him. Wait for me here. Quick twenty bucks, then I'm outta here and we can go get some beer."

I knew Steffin sold himself to older men for money, but I never expected to go with him and stand guard.

"I'm a minor, so I can't get caught in the bar," he said. "I won't be long. If you see any cops, bang on the window. And don't stare through the glass, Cinderella. You look out of place!"

"No kidding!" I was so uncomfortable.

Steffin finally came outside with forty dollars in his fingers, all smiles. "Did two," he said, grabbing me by the shirt. We ran toward the nearest depanneur. "You could do it, too, Jo. There's always an adult wanting to buy sex from a kid."

Steffin opened the door to the depanneur and we went in. We walked up and down the alcohol section filled with cheap wine and beer.

"Isn't there another way to make forty bucks?" I looked at the produce in the aisles of the store as we casually talked about child prostitution, though somehow it seemed normal. It was our normal.

"I make more money sucking dick than anything else I could do. Who's gonna hire me, Jo?" Steffin grabbed a six-pack of beer.

We drank in a deserted parking lot behind an apartment building. I pulled a half-smoked joint tucked inside tinfoil from my cigarette pack and lit it. "You could be a personal dresser," I said.

"Code for cocksucker."

"You could work as a babysitter!"

"Then I'd have to suck the father's dick."

I told him that not every man wanted him to suck his cock, but then he described how a police officer had raped him in the back seat of a cruiser when he was twelve years old. He was busted for prostitution. It seemed bizarre, arresting a twelve-year-old after adult males had had sex with him.

"You were raped by a cop?" I asked. Up until that point, I had thought of officers as people who kept order, not as people who raped little boys. "Did you ever tell on him?"

"Tell who? They're the cops. They're the ones you're supposed to tell."

I squeezed in closer to Steffin, tucked strands of his long blond hair behind his ear, and wrapped my arms around his midsection. After he smoked the last few hits of the joint, he smothered the heater and hugged me back. We just held each other as if neither of us had been hugged in years.

We made our way to the monument in the park at the foot of Mount Royal where Steffin usually looked for gay men cruising along the paths, a hot spot for nightly encounters.

I sat on the concrete stairs beside one of the four green lions and stared up at the monument; above me was a figure with wings. Steffin took out a pill bottle and swallowed a blue pill with his beer. He gave me one.

"I think your mother has a thing for Clint," Steffin said.

I socked him in the arm, hard. Steffin always pushed people, crossed a line verbally. It was his habit, and he liked to get reactions out of people. My mother hated him. Many adults were turned off by him, but I always thought it was because they were homophobic. But I would not discuss my mother or anything sexual with him. That was off-limits. "You shut the fuck up." I punched him again.

"Okay!" Steff said. He put the cap back on the pill bottle.

I straddled the green lion, my face resting against the cold metal. Steff was lying down on the stairs below me. I touched my belly under my shirt, pinched my waist, a habit of checking for fat. We heard the voices of two police officers approaching us. We got up and ran, chased off the grounds by them.

"Rapers!" I screamed over and over, until we were both screaming "Rapers!" at the top of our lungs while our hearts raced and we couldn't catch our breath between running and raging, late for rehearsal.

Our troupe was rehearsing a new play. We jammed, strummed guitars, recited poetry, and pretended we were members of the Beat Generation, painting on walls as if they were giant canvases.

After rehearsal, Splash wanted to go to the park with Georgia, Steffin, and me.

"What about me?" Clint asked. His hair was matted. He had showed up late for rehearsal that day, drunk.

"You can come if you want but you have to wipe that look off your mug," Splash said as he studied himself in a mirror, puckering his lips. He always looked so beautiful compared to the rest of us with his carefully chosen wardrobe, sparkling eyeshadow, and multicoloured fingernails.

Clint blurted out that he wasn't going to hang out with us *faggots* anymore and that he was quitting the show. I ran after him into the stairwell and grabbed hold of his arm. He tried to put his arms around my waist, but he smelled like beer, so I pushed him away. He grabbed me by the arm, pulled me back toward him, then pushed me down the stairs when I tried to get away from him. I stumbled down and landed on the stone landing. Clint ran down to see if I was okay, but I smacked him and screamed at him to fuck off and leave me alone.

"Please don't leave me. I don't know what's wrong with me. I don't know." He was crying. I had never seen Clint cry.

I had never told him about my father and he never asked, so he didn't know about the childhood of violence, or understand that he had done something we could never recover from.

"I'm sorry," Clint said.

I pulled away when he reached for me. His reflexes weren't as fast with booze in him.

"Fucking … come here!" he screamed.

I left him on the stairs as quickly as I could. Georgia, Steff, and Splash were huddled behind a door, listening. I heard them whispering: *asshole, caveman, Homo sapien.*

When I got home my mother was waiting for me. She held my journal in her fingers. I ran to my room to see my belongings scattered everywhere.

"You're doing drugs," she declared.

I screamed at my mother while she stood in the doorway to my room. I tore my journal out of her hands and threw it on my bed.

"You live under my roof, missy, and I have the right to check and make sure —"

"No, you don't. It's my journal. Get out of my fucking room!" I pushed her.

"Don't you dare shove me. Are you trying to hurt me?"

I used both of my hands and pushed her a second time, in the chest, until she stumbled back. Then I slammed the door.

Everything seemed to fall apart that day. My relationship with Clint was over. He wasn't the same boy.

I later walked by her bedroom, where she was lying on her bed. She saw me staring at her. "Please come here. Come sit with me."

I didn't move, could barely look at her. Hearing those words always made me feel ill, just like when she said "I love you." I hated it when she asked me to go closer to her or sit with her, particularly if she was on a bed or the couch.

A number of weeks went by. Clint and my mother spoke several times on the telephone, something I found weird and unbearable. Then Clint showed up at our rehearsal studio looking for me. He had stubble on his face and wore dirty clothes, smelled of booze and cigarettes. He had bandages on his hands up to his wrists.

We walked to the park in the snow. We huddled together in a gazebo. Clint unwrapped his bandage and showed me a large gash on the palm of his hand. He had broken a beer bottle and cut his palm with it.

"I think I'll kill myself if we don't get back together."

I gently rubbed my finger over his cut, rubbed the exposed flesh to keep it warm, then let go of his palm as a group of children came charging past us, making big footprints in the snow and dropping down to make snow angels before running off.

"I gotta get back," I said, wanting to get back to rehearsal and away from him. He was lost somehow, broken. I wished I could have helped him, or picked up his heart to put it back in his chest. I wished he could be the same arrogant, confident kid I had met that first time, with a smoke tucked behind his ear and that smug smile. He wasn't that boy anymore.

I said goodbye and left.

# CHAPTER TWELVE

I WAS FOURTEEN and had found a new look: thick black eye-liner and black clothes (shoes, socks, jeans, and shirts). I decided I was grown and would make my own decisions — to cut classes, get high, drink, steal.

Mother became less and less interested in parenting and couldn't force me to follow her rules. The more I pushed the boundaries, the more she let go. I didn't realize that she had already given up.

It was a Friday night like any other. I walked into the kitchen to get a drink. My mother was at the table with a pen and notebook.

"We are going to Toronto. There's a school there and I think it could be a good place for you," Mother said casually. "It has a theatre program. What do you think?" she asked, as if my opinion mattered.

I grunted, lifted my shoulders to my ears. I had known the day was coming — the day she would get rid of me — so it wasn't so much a surprise. Maybe she thought she would get a fight. She looked half ready for one, but I walked to the fridge and pulled a can of soda out. "Toronto is fine," I said. I opened the can, watching it fizz over as I inhaled and sipped at the bubbles before sauntering to my room.

End of discussion.

I heard Mother on the phone, squawking away like Charlie Brown's teacher. I didn't care anymore. It had been building ever since she ransacked my bedroom, looking for reasons to send me off. I preferred New York, but Toronto would do. She'd been trying to find a place for me to go for nearly a year, and maybe this one would stick. What I hadn't figured out was why. Why had my mother been trying to find a place to send me? It wasn't that I didn't want to get away from her — I did, but I must have been just horrible enough for her to want to get me out. I smoked, I drank, I cursed. I actively hated her. I was an adolescent and needed help. Instead, I was being sent away as if it were normal.

Steffin, Splash, Georgia, and I sat in my living room listening to Roberta Flack, sipping wine and holding on to each other. It was the last time we would be together.

"Splash, you gotta change your name to something else," I said. "Splash sounds like the name of a dolphin or something."

We all laughed, including Splash. Fish face. Crabby cakes. Sharky. Flipper.

"Call yourself Flipper," Georgia snorted.

I was going to miss this group. Georgia and I cried and held on to each other.

"We'll always be sisters," she said.

"Yeah, we'll always all be sisters," Steffin joined in.

Splash was almost a "sister," and people called Steffin a girl because he was gay. We all just accepted the insults from horrible people. We thought they were small-minded idiots. We were arrogant teens, luckily, or else the pain of our lives would have taken each one of us down.

We stayed on the couch and held each other like a family of animals, limbs over limbs, bodies entwined. I kissed Georgia on the lips and she kissed me back, gently, my favourite part of goodbye.

"I'm going to have to visit you," Steffin said the next morning as I carried my luggage to the car and hoisted it into the trunk.

It was hot out. I wiped the sweat off my forehead with the back of my hand after closing the trunk and stared at Steffin. "I can't imagine not being able to cruise the streets with you," I said, smirking.

My mother was still in the washroom, so we sat on the curb for a minute.

"I got you something," he said and pulled out a picture of himself. "Oh, and this ..." He reached into his jacket pocket and produced a few pills wrapped in foil.

"Not sure how I'll cope without waiting for you outside seedy bars, Steffin."

"I'm sure you'll figure it out, though not sure how you'll get along without me," he said.

"I'm not so sure either, Steff. Please visit soon. I mean, a couple of cocks and you should have enough money for a bus ticket, right?" We laughed and hugged.

My mother came out of the door in her floral-patterned dress, with full makeup on, carrying her purse and a flash camera, which dangled from her wrist like a bracelet.

"We have to go. I didn't know you would be here, Steffin," Mother said with disdain as she made her way around us to the driver's door. Steffin and I both noticed that her dress was tucked inside her pantyhose at the back, exposing a large portion of her backside.

"Hey, Helen, honey, I can see your moon," Steffin said.

"Don't honey me, Steffin, it's rude," she said. She had never liked him, but couldn't rip us apart no matter how hard she tried. "Come on, Joanne, get in the car, please. We have to go. Say goodbye, and lord, isn't one goodbye enough? How many days in a row do you need to say goodbye?" she said in a mini-rant as she pulled her dress out of her pantyhose.

I hugged Steffin.

I would see him soon enough. I would travel on the overnight train from Toronto to Montreal on weekends to continue rehearsals for our play. We were going to be heading out across Canada on tour, and the Adelaide Court Theatre in Toronto would be the first stop after Montreal.

"I'll see you soon," I said, and pulled away from our embrace.

"Yeah ... get laid, will ya, Jo?" he said as he walked away from me, flipping his hair like Cher as he walked down the road.

I sat in the car with my mother, and for the first time there was no bickering as we listened to music on the radio from Montreal to Toronto, knowing it would be our last couple of days together. The transition was strange. I kept waiting for my mother to say something like "If you need me just call," or any number of things, but she said nothing. It was as if she were dropping me off at a rehearsal or a lesson. I was the last to be deposited, falling off like a button from a shirt — all four of her children would be gone, and she would have nothing left to hold her in. She would be free. I was almost fifteen and this was it. Lou and Sadie had been removed and she didn't shed a tear. There were never any tears, only tiny victories for her, it seemed. We were the weight of her suffering somehow, reflections of her younger self perhaps, and for whatever reason, she wanted us gone.

With my departure she was able to tell people how her daughter had been accepted into an arts school in Toronto, but it was only a facade. This had been a year in the making, my exit, her flight.

There was little more to say except goodbye. Strange, I felt nothing.

Goodbye, Mother.

# Broken

## PART TWO

# CHAPTER THIRTEEN

## 2002 — Princess Margaret Hospital

MOTHER SITS UP in her hospital bed talking with her social worker. The sound of the ocean comes from a CD in her beat box. I stop just outside her room, away from them. I don't want to interrupt, and I don't want to be part of something intimate. I can hear them talking about her journey from the West Coast. My mother is telling this woman about the people she lived with on Indigenous land in British Columbia, her home before she came here.

I hide around the corner and think about the circuitous route Mother took to get to Toronto. It began only months ago as I looked down over the wing of the plane, sunlight bounced off the snowy pines of the Rocky Mountains in the heart of British Columbia. I was going to see my mother for the very first time in fifteen years. I wondered what it had been like for my mother to fly nearly five thousand kilometres west when she left us. I was no longer the fourteen-year-old she had left, but a thirty-one-year-old woman. She was no longer forty-seven, but sixty-two. She had adjusted to a life so far removed from the early days, from my youth.

I imagined her home in Bella Coola by the river in Nuxalk territory. I'd only seen it in pictures: the salmon stream, old-growth forests, and grizzly bears. Three thousand people lived in that beautiful valley. There were only two ways into it. One, on a small plane that holds no more than ten people, and the other, on a long road, built by the locals back in the 1950s, where one wrong turn of the steering wheel could send you to the bottom of the valley. This killer highway in and out of the reserve was called Freedom Road.

My mother had left Montreal after she met an Indigenous man, and after she pilfered five thousand dollars from the plastic factory she worked for as the accountant. She also stole the cash from a pyramid scheme after getting friends and family to invest. She left unpaid telephone and electric bills and just vanished. I learned about the pyramid from Martha because she had gone in on it, as did another friend of hers, a well-known news anchor at the time. I felt guilty for that and ended up giving fifteen hundred dollars from my earnings to Martha to give to the journalist.

Mother was apparently working for the Nuxalk, collecting government grants on behalf of the band. She founded her own company, New Era, and created programs for children, teaching dance lessons from our old vinyl albums, the same records I had learned from with Miss Kristy. It was a wonder how she could do it. She hadn't been able to walk very far when I was a kid because she would struggle for breath, but somehow, after never having danced, she was able to teach. She knew all the steps, the shuffles and flaps and time steps. She had instructions and old lesson books with diagrams. She had memories of all those years watching us. Her desire to dance had never faded; she just found a way to plant little tapping dreams into other children.

Remarkable, really.

She had created a whole new persona in BC, a woman I didn't know who seemed to be held in high esteem for her efforts on the reserve. She lived tax free and lied about her Indigenous status, claiming to be half Mohawk. Maybe she did have some Mohawk in her, but it was news to me. She lost the man but continued to live on the reserve, taking twenty percent of the government grant funds as income, with the rest going to the band, chief, and town.

While I knew the community she lived in and the people she served in Bella Coola appreciated her, they did not know the woman who had escaped Montreal with other people's money, the woman who got rid of her children, one by one, and created programs for a village of kids while her own still struggled to survive.

I was flying in to see her, in spite of everything, because she had stage four cancer. She had waited five years before seeking treatment for her symptoms, hemorrhaging, losing large quantities of blood. She was afraid to go to doctors, maybe depressed or on her own suicide mission.

I checked in to my hotel, aware that I would be seeing Lou and Diego, who had also flown out. Not Sadie. She didn't want to see our mother, and no one blamed her. Mother was having an operation at Vancouver General Hospital and had been airlifted out of the valley of Bella Coola. I wouldn't see her home on the reserve, and she would never see mine. I didn't want her to see how I lived, in an apartment cluttered with belongings I had dragged along from my adolescent years — a trunk, a vintage wine-stained table. Books were scattered about, papers everywhere — notes to self, quotes that motivated, art from friends. It was personal, my nest.

After a long embrace and rounds of hellos with Lou and me, my brother stayed downstairs on the main floor of the hospital to find his lost wallet. Upstairs, Lou and I linked arms outside our mother's hospital room door. We stared at each other. My stomach was sore with that familiar feeling of dread. Our mother would be in a bed, vulnerable. I had no idea what to expect, only that I didn't want to lose myself.

Lou squeezed my arm. "Let's do it."

We paused to stare at the door once more before pushing it open.

Mother cried and stretched out her arms for us. I didn't know how to ignore her physical request for affection, and it was too late to run. We hugged her briefly, then stood on either side of her bed.

"Look at you both. Lou, your hair is the same, red and curly as ever."

"Yours too," Lou said.

Mother looked the same: her hair was shoulder length and chestnut brown, and her large frame was wrapped in blankets. I breathed in that distinctive and familiar body odour, the decaying smell of unbathed adult skin.

"Look at you, Joanne. You're so pretty and thin."

Of course she mentioned my weight. Mother was frail but not fragile; she still weighed hundreds of pounds. Being thin was not a conversation I wanted to have with her. There was silence in the room. No one knew what to say, but I was seething. It had taken thirty seconds for her to focus on my weight. It had been so long since we had seen each other, and yet maybe she didn't know how else to bridge the divide.

I took a deep breath, closed and opened my eyes as calmly as I could while I screamed *Get off me!* in my head. I exhaled, looked at her without expression, and reminded myself, *I am grown; she has cancer.* I would give her nothing but these moments of my time. My body weight would not be a topic of discussion. In fact, I was off-limits entirely.

We shifted in place. Lou took a seat as far from our mother as possible. I stayed standing, trying to come up with a reason to bolt. But this was what it was — awkward moments, talk of hair, weight, illness, until she was wheeled away for a dangerous operation.

Five hours later the doctors came to talk to us in the waiting room. They had removed the tumour successfully, but the cancer was advanced. It had metastasized, spread to other organs. The most they could do was treat the symptoms with radiation or chemotherapy. Give her a year, two at most, to live. She was dying. After a fifteen-year separation. Fifteen years was a long time.

Fifteen years *is* a long time.

There's a common belief that the cells in our body regenerate twice in fifteen years. In those fifteen years, 185 full moons had risen and the twentieth century had turned into the twenty-first. In those fifteen years my mother had left behind a series of disasters in Montreal, left behind her family, embedded herself in a new community, created a new life. She had escaped the law. But in the end, she hadn't escaped her children.

I stood right in front of her, with a history visible on my flesh and body, in the spaces where time got stuck, halted, and in the scars and lines that developed over time.

Mother packed up her life in Bella Coola with the help of friends and Diego. She left her surrogate daughters and sons on the reserve, her students and programs, so she could live close to Diego and me in Toronto, where she would live out the remainder of her days.

I hear my name, which calls me back to the present. She is talking to the social worker about me. I try not to hear what is being spoken, but I know it's about those early days, of tap shoes and lessons, when Mother ingested it all for her future role as teacher. I back up even farther, trying not to be seen, but it's too late. They see movement and call my name. I step inside the door frame as if I've just arrived.

"I can come back if you're busy or need more time," I say.

"No, we're done. I'll leave you two to visit," the social worker says. "You can call me anytime. I'm right down the hall," she says to my mother.

Mother, wiping tears from her eyes, thanks the social worker as she leaves. I don't ask if she is okay. I fidget with my bag and wind my earphones, putting them away.

"I told her a little about the dancing days and how much I loved it, how good you were."

I try to steer the conversation away from me, "You taught dance, right, to the children in Bella Coola? How did you teach them?" We both know I am asking how it was possible since she never danced and could barely move. She couldn't even walk a block back in the day.

"Mostly I just played those old albums and taught them how to flap and shuffle and even time step. I suppose I danced," Mother says, "but not much."

I have a hard time imagining her teaching dance to a cluster of kids, but she did it. It was a little absurd, but nothing with my mother is unthinkable. She is quite brilliant, really, savvy. She even, it turns out, ran her own restaurant on the reserve in BC, called Homesteaders, serving lasagna and french fries in a place where people fished for wild salmon and picked mushrooms from the land.

"I did dance, and those records had fantastic instructions." She smiles.

I have to give it to her. She is smart, courageous even, and somehow found the confidence to teach dance to children, though she weighs at least four hundred pounds by now.

"Well, that's something, especially given that your mother wouldn't let you dance," I say as we look warily at each other.

"You were a good dancer," she says.

I think of the days when she carted me everywhere for shows and lessons, or when she needed me, when she would not let me go and I couldn't get away. I am not ready to speak about this, not yet. Instead I ask about my father once more.

"How old were you when you met Domenic?" I ask.

"My father knew your dad, you know, from a construction site. It's how I met your father. He was so handsome then. He looked like he could have been a model in a magazine, with his black hair and those green eyes." Mom sits up in her hospital bed. "I was seventeen and I got pregnant. Your grandfather wanted me to get married."

"What happened when Sadie was a baby?"

My mother's face drops as she fiddles with her blanket and slowly exhales.

"I didn't want to marry anyone and I didn't want to have a baby," she whispers. I wait through the silence, allow it, hope it will carry us to a common space where we can hear each other. I sit close to her and wrap my arms around my waist for comfort.

"What happened after Sadie was born?"

My mother picks up one of her teddy bears and holds it on her belly as she continues to speak calmly. "I told everyone that Sadie died at birth.... But I couldn't stand it and wanted her back, so I picked her up from the foster home. There were six babies in that home. So cute." She speaks in a slow measured tone.

"How long was Sadie there?"

"Six months."

"People thought she was dead for six months?" I ask.

"Yeah, and then I had to explain to my cousins and parents what happened, why I suddenly had a baby."

"Is that why your father wanted you to marry Dad?"

My mother coughs and reaches for her water glass. I grab the cup and hold it close to her mouth while she drinks from the straw. She clears her throat and continues.

"Your father and I lived with my parents for three years after we got Sadie back." She looks at me, her eyes glossy, filled with such sadness.

"I didn't know you told people Sadie died."

"Yeah. Maybe I should have left her in the foster home. Maybe I should have left."

I don't tell her that she did leave, though not before shoving us out the door like a once-loved Christmas tree stripped bare of all the bells and baubles, tinsel and lights, and left on the curb.

"We were just kids," I say under my breath, more to myself than to her.

"You were so cute. You were a good girl …"

She looks too closely at me. I want to run now, but I stay. There is a pause. We look at each other, and somehow it's as if she knows what I am about to say.

"I need to know, Mom. Why?" I call her Mom, but I don't mean to. It slips out. "Why did you do what you did to me?"

She knows exactly what I mean even though I don't know how to get the words out. But she doesn't skip a beat. Her face hardens with defensiveness, and that wagging finger flies up into the air, pointing right at me. And before she speaks, I also know what she is going to say, so I close my heart very quickly to avoid the toxic, dismissive response.

"I never touched you."

I shut down, look away. I know she is not inside herself. I can't reach her. I want to; it's what I've always wanted to do, understand, make sense of my life, but she will not meet my needs. She will not come clean, ever. I ask a new question.

"Why did you let him beat us?" I look right at her again. This time I am prepared for her slippery reply.

"I didn't let him. He was … I should have stopped him. You're right."

Not good enough. Sadist, she set it up most of the time. She must think I can't remember my own history, as she tries to rewrite it and wipe the slate.

I hear the word in my head again: *Mom*. I don't speak. I tell myself that it's okay as I walk to lift the blinds and let more sunlight into the dark space that has enveloped me. The ocean music is still playing. I turn it off.

"Oh … I liked that," Mother says.

A man clanks in with a tray of food. "Dinnertime," he says, then disappears.

I walk around my mother's bed to grab the tray, lift the lid to expose her soup in a cup, mashed potatoes, and some type of meat with brown gravy.

"I can't eat that," she says.

The fluorescent light flickers above us, making me feel dizzy. I rub my eyes. The air in the room is dry and I'm tired. Mother changes the subject again.

"I could go for a slice of pie or a milkshake," she says. "My mother used to bake butterscotch pies. One day there were seven pies cooling on the rack in the kitchen and I stole one, ate the whole thing right under the kitchen table. My mother found me and gave me a beating for it. I did it all the time, though. Couldn't stop myself from stealing a butterscotch pie." Mother looks at me. She stares at my body. I am aware of it and begin to twitch in my seat. "I loved eating those pies as much as you loved eating air, eating nothing," she finishes, referencing the subject I've been trying to avoid: my life-and-death struggle with anorexia that developed after I moved by myself to Toronto as a teen.

I don't want to talk about food or the lack of it, but I'm pulled into it.

"I ate air because sometimes I had no choice." I know it's not entirely true, but there were days when I couldn't afford to eat, when I stole or did worse so I could eat.

"You were sick."

"That's not what I said." I look down at my hands. I want to say *Stop, please stop.* I want to say, *I was just a girl when you left me in a new city. I said goodbye to my friends and hometown. I lost everything.* But I can't say these things; she won't hear me. She won't give me the very little I look for — some truth, some peace. I just want her to say, *I shouldn't have touched you. I shouldn't have left you. I shouldn't have let your dad beat you. I shouldn't have done the things I did. I'm sorry.* It's not too much to ask before she dies, I don't think, but she won't do it.

If you excavated my mother's heart, you would find the remains of her children.

And all I can get out is "I have an audition." It's a lie, but I stand up to look at my watch. I lift the blanket over her midsection to tuck her in.

She looks at me quietly, then smiles. "Oh, what for?"

I lie some more. "Cartoon," I say as I pick up my backpack. "Voice work."

"Can you put the ocean on again before you leave?"

I push the on button and the sound of rushing water fills the room once more.

# CHAPTER FOURTEEN

## 1983

TORONTO WAS A CITY I didn't understand. There were no depanneurs stocked with wine, beer, and Gitanes cigarettes, no smell of bakeries and bagels. No all-night bar parties or graffiti art taking over the city walls or the lyrical voices of francophones. I had no solid roots in the glass and concrete city of Toronto. It was cold — abrupt, almost, if a city could be abrupt, like my departure from Montreal had been.

My mother had rented the space from an advertisement in the paper before we drove here. The apartment was sparsely furnished. No cluttered corners, candles, or knick-knacks. A beige apartment. Barry was my roommate, a musician from the Montreal theatre who worked with Martha. We rarely saw each other, and Martha would come weekly to develop a show. It was the plan, to go to school and rehearse on occasional weekends, but I felt like a displaced child, a refugee in a new land.

I wanted to nestle with Steffin under trees during the Tam Tam Jam drumming on the mountain, play records and sing badly, or visit with Lou. I wanted the familiar mayhem with my friends, a life known to me — what subway stop was mine, who I might run into, controlling the day's fate, knowing where I would land at night and that the next day I would have friends and the familiar *je ne sais quoi*. I knew nothing of Toronto, only that my new school was one block away. My world was suddenly condensed to school and the apartment.

I attended the Toronto High School for the Performing Arts. Our entire school took up the second floor of a brownstone building on Adelaide Street, right across from the Goodwill on Jarvis Street and above a dance school. It was a very small building, no signs or glitter, just a two-flight walk-up for roughly one hundred students. Windows lined the walls in every room. There were wooden floors and mirrors for dance students. The program included theatre, dance, and music.

My apartment was a block away from Saint James Park, which spanned the space between my apartment and the school and was home to many homeless people, with their bottles, carts, and sleeping bags. I didn't venture out at night. During the day, I just focused on the pavement between my apartment and school as I dealt with everything that was new, especially teachers and students — people who had homes and families.

On my first day, I wore a fedora, black boots, thick eyeliner. I kept my hands in my pockets and a smoke dangling from my mouth, trying so hard to be cool, to hide my eyes.

Ms. Kate was my academic teacher. She was from Australia. If accents themselves could be friendly, Australian was the friendliest. Ms. Kate had a buzz cut and wore pants and sneakers and eyeliner that made her green eyes pop. That first day was difficult because there was no place for me to hide. There were four of us sitting at a large table in a small room, looking up at Ms. Kate, our teacher for humanities and social sciences. Afternoons were for our chosen art discipline. Mine was the theatre program, with students from grades eight to thirteen, about thirty-five in total, in a large room that looked out over the park on Jarvis Street. We would all come to spend very intimate time with each other, like it or not.

The mornings were impossible in the beginning. Along with social awkwardness came enormous insecurity around my reading and writing. I could not read at the same level as the other students. I had failed grade eight in Montreal, but skipped a grade and went into grade ten in Toronto. My reading level was that of a twelve-year-old. I could not lie, hide, or cheat without getting caught.

Ms. Kate started to worry about me. It began in my fourth detention. I was two weeks in with no homework to show. I was alone in our classroom, no bigger than a small office, the sounds of cars from Adelaide Street mixing with the pounding rain. I was the only one in detention when Kate walked in, and I buried my face in my book, pretending to read. She came to sit beside me, asking me how I was, and all I could do was cry.

"I don't know. I don't know how to read this book quickly. I can't keep up," I said without looking at her. And after two weeks of my trying to fit in and navigate not only living alone in a new city, but new kids and no space of comfort anywhere, Kate put one hand atop mine and held my shoulder with the other hand. It unleashed a torrent. I tried to speak, but my words only came out in whispers and heaving cries like a little child's. I was embarrassed but couldn't stop myself. She hugged me and said it was okay, that we could go slowly, that she would give me different assignments until I caught up to the same level of reading and writing as the others. But she knew it was more than the ABCs that made me cry so uncontrollably.

After that detention, Ms. Kate watched out for me. In the morning she would ask, "How is the apartment?" or "Did you have breakfast today?" I normally said "Okay" or "Yes," but in those first few weeks I became acutely aware of the silence, the nighttime stillness that engulfed the apartment when I was alone at home. The seclusion, the unrelenting loneliness, created a growing misery, a constant pain. After a few weeks, though, it became normal, like a broken bone that never heals.

As well, my past intruded: a constant tap of memory that I could not turn off. And I couldn't turn down the volume inside my head. It was like a radio left on, with the words *fat, bitch, unlovable* repeating themselves. And in my isolation, I developed a new routine — standing in front of the mirror while alone in my room, I stared at my face, arms, hips, legs, dissecting body parts. I wondered what it was about the body that people obsessed over, its thinness or thickness, colour of eyes, hair, where a nose sat on a face, marks, scars, breasts.

I was lonely. And the new routine that started as distraction became an obsession. I spent my time wondering how I could lose weight, and I ate less and less as I continually examined my own flesh. I avoided Barry when possible. He didn't seem to notice my behaviour, and it wasn't his job to pay attention or babysit. We were roommates.

I didn't know how to cook or which nutrients a growing body needed. In Montreal, I didn't have to buy groceries or clean and cook. Those were my mother's chores. In Toronto, they were mine. It was overwhelming and I ignored a lot of my basic needs: haircuts, shoe shopping, dental visits.

After each day filled with the energy of young people, music, dance, and theatre, I went home to a tiny apartment in the sky with only clouds as company until the moon rose. Nights were a nightmare. My flashbacks were becoming regular, and any loud sound might set me off: an ambulance, a thunderclap, shouting from the street. I ended up in the bathroom one night, hitting my head against the cabinet beneath the sink while I sat on the cold tile floor. I could not stop the internal chaos, an audience of sounds, of voices and visuals. I didn't know there was such a thing as mental illness — a condition with a treatment. I only thought I was crazy, and I was trying to stop it. I did pick up the large yellow telephone book one night and looked up the heading "Help." There was nothing. I paced, looked out the window to the sky, and talked out loud to myself to drown out the images and noises inside my head. Then I discovered a new coping strategy. I positioned a standing mirror against the wall, close to my pillow, to help me sleep. I was my own pseudo-friend. It was a strange comfort.

I did slowly let down my guard at school. It was far more fun than any other school I had been to, with music, art, and teens who wore ripped clothes and jewels, had coloured hair, and didn't bully. They were students who didn't fit the mainstream, artists or kids who wanted to become famous, or wealthy kids like pimply John, who lived in the Bridle Path and flew helicopters with his father to pick up Schwartz's smoked meat in Montreal when they were in the mood. He tried to buy friendship as much as I tried to stay away from relationships.

With only four students in my classroom, it was hard to truly ignore people, particularly Jasmine. She was black and wore the same grey checkered coat, which covered her large frame, to school every day. She was the biggest girl in school, one of three black students and wickedly bright. She was also the most adorable, but she had a mean stare if she was mad, which made me laugh, and she would laugh with me while others retreated. I became her friend. We both understood something about the other — that we had our armour that others could not recognize or understand. We were drawn to each other, radical opposites in some ways, but so much alike: obsessed with Michael Jackson, poetry, street art, and cryptic talk about parents and adults.

"There is a guy in my building that wants me to prostitute. He's always around. My mother works the night shift," Jasmine said.

I connected the dots and responded, "My mother was a bloodsucker, and my father was a prick." Sometimes I told people my parents were dead, and it made them stop asking personal questions, but with Jasmine it was different.

We were also both obsessed with food. She overate, while I starved. We both counted calories. She counted the thousands she consumed, while I counted the ones I didn't.

I was hungry all the time. I thought of all the foods I wanted to eat, like pizza, macaroni, ice cream. I didn't let people know I was hungry. It was private and I didn't want to fail at losing weight, fail because I was hungry. I wanted to hear hunger, the rumble inside my stomach, like the coo of a dove. I decided to succeed at being hungry. Mastering hunger meant I could control and do anything I put my mind to.

I would lie on my back and touch my stomach as one of my "fat tests," and after many weeks my belly slowly melted like snow, in line with my hipbones, flat. But still I thought I was fat. My reflection in the mirror became an actual companion, an internal voice that scolded me.

I would open the fridge and stare at Barry's food — the cheese, eggs, and meat I wouldn't dare eat. I would stand in front of the mirror in my bedroom, take all my clothes off, and pinch the flesh on my stomach. It reminded me of my mother, her words, her obsession, her size.

"Good for nothing," my mother used to call Sadie and Lou. "You want to be like your sisters, Joanne?" I knew what she meant, the words she often said about my sisters: *fat, lazy, good-for-nothings*. Every pinch of flesh on my frame was like a direct line to her wagging finger, her intrusive, silent stare.

I wondered how many calories I could consume and still lose weight. I would stand in front of the mirror and run in place on the beige carpet, whispering words in rhythm, in my bare feet. *Fatso, fatso, fatso.* It was a silly jingle, but I believed if I kept moving I would lose weight. I could even lose time. I could lose myself, if I just kept moving.

A meal included an apple with cheese or a muffin, toast and peanut butter, or tin soup. I stopped eating meat right away. The thought of anything dying for my consumption made me ill. I made up numbers, exaggerated caloric intake. A muffin equalled four hundred calories. A slice of cheese, three hundred. Soup, five hundred. An apple, one hundred. I kept my caloric intake under twelve hundred per day. I had seen this number on the cover of a magazine where I bought my food, at Loblaws in an underground mall on Yonge Street. Apple. Muffin. Cheese. Soup. I would choose three of those items per day, rotating through them. Sometimes I ate a banana. I would slice it thinly and eat it slowly, pretending it was a large meal, that a banana equalled four hundred calories.

"You've lost weight, Joanne," Martha said on one of her weekend visits, proud of me for the accomplishment. I knew she would be. I waited for her praise.

"Come," she said, standing in front of the mirror in the bedroom, ushering me over with her hands. "Come here."

She wanted me to stand in front of her while she placed her hands on my hips as we looked at each other in the mirror's reflection.

"Wow, you've lost your hips, your bum, they're gone. God, you look amazing." I had never heard Martha say that I looked amazing before. "How did you do it?" She rubbed my torso, feeling for signs of fat, her fingers moving up and down my body.

"I don't know," I lied, while her hands fell over my bum and thighs and moved back up to my waist.

"Well, you look fantastic."

Martha's pleasure over my appearance excited me, changed the relationship somehow. Was this all it took? Hunger? Being skinny?

Martha took over the apartment just as she did every room she entered. I wasn't used to sharing my bed, but it was only for the occasional weekend, and I didn't mind the break from the routine of starvation and quiet nights. The drill sergeant's commands and insults inside my head would be drowned out with Martha's non-stop talk, reminders of the old life I had tried to escape, bringing news of my mother along with Montreal bagels and wine. My excitement would turn to exhaustion, and I would wait for her to finally leave, leaving me alone with my mirror, beige walls, and routines. The routines were all that held me together, as if putting pressure on a gushing vein.

"Let's exercise. You can show me how you lost the weight." She wanted to do what I did and so we ran around the apartment, jumping on the beige carpet to Simon and Garfunkel or Cat Stevens. The next time she visited, she stared at me again, wrapping her hands around my waist, pushing her flat hand onto my belly. Her obsession with my body seemed odd, and also sensual, but Martha never had boundaries, and she wanted others to be infatuated with her. I wasn't anymore; that had faded along with my weight. But it seemed the more I lost, the more I was loved, and, real or not, it was what I perceived. It took a while to understand that Martha was measuring her own body size and shape against mine and trying to lose weight as I had. She was beginning to reduce caloric intake as well, and every time she visited she would do the same things.

On one of the visits, my mother arrived with her.

"You've got to stop. It's too much now, Joanne. Too thin," Mother said, sitting at the table in the dining area.

"Well, which is it? I thought I was fat," I said in a soft conversational tone.

Mother smirked and didn't seem to mind the banter. Her mounds of fat sagged over the chair she sat on like an umbrella. She was physically larger, had gained weight.

Her scent, like food rotting in a refrigerator, filled the apartment, and I had to stop myself from gagging. She always made me feel like I wanted to be small enough to disappear, become a ghost.

"Enough is enough, Joanne. You're like a bird."

"I like birds." I flapped my arms, bent them at the elbow like a chicken, and smiled.

I wanted them gone, Martha and my mother. All I wanted to do was lie down. What became clear was how separate they were from my new Toronto life, from Kate, Jasmine, my day to day. Martha and my mother were like the dead coming to life. They reminded me of all that had been, made me want to rip them apart, both of them. I hated them, but they did not know it.

# CHAPTER FIFTEEN

DAYS LATER I SAW an ad in the paper: Brad Fraser was auditioning actors for his play *Wolfboy* in the basement of a church on Queen Street West. I didn't know anything about the script, but after school I made my way to the streetcar, going over the words of the contemporary monologue I had done at Juilliard.

I was cast and over the moon. The play was performed at Toronto's famous Theatre Passe Muraille and I was able to work with Shirley Douglas, mother bear to all Canadians, who watched out for me and gave me advice. And Keanu Reeves, a boy who helped fix my bicycle one day when my tire blew. Sweetest kid. He reminded me of an energized puppy, full of life and eager to learn, finding his way in the world, like I was. We were two teenagers adrift, working hard. He had also gone to my performing arts school but left before I started.

My character in the play was dead, a ghost who had been raped and murdered and was now haunting her killer. I was running on empty, though, playing the dead girl every night, screaming, walking through walls, and "reliving" the rape and murder every night while haunting my killer. My mental health was not improving with the part. Ghost Girl began to seep into my days and it was hard to shake the role.

I went to school after a few days of work. At lunchtime, the entire school was in the theatre room, listening to the theme song from *Fame*, leaping off windowsills, dancing on tables. I wanted to dance but was too self-conscious, so instead I watched from the corner until Kate came and found me.

"Joanne, we have to talk," Kate said, ushering me to her office. "I want you to meet someone, a woman I know. She's a healer."

"You mean some type of social worker?" I didn't trust adults who spoke to kids to earn a living; they were the ones who took children away.

"No. She's a healer, has a private practice, someone people talk with." Kate and I sat in her office. She was the only adult I wanted to talk to; even talking with people my own age was becoming a challenge. I didn't want to go to teen parties, to eat chips or pizza while kids guzzled beer in backyards when parents were absent. I had done those things in Montreal. I was not living a child's life and didn't need to hide my drug use or hunger. I was on my own.

"I can drive you to meet her, see if you like her," Ms. Kate said. "Think about it."

I didn't want to talk to a healer. The idea terrified me, as if she might discover how fucked up I was. "I don't have time right now," I said, which was true. School and the play were more than I could manage.

"Just think about it. There is always time to talk," she said.

But I still rejected the idea, even after the run of *Wolfboy* ended and I was back to school, and back to my routines.

The reality of having no home was sinking in. I was falling into a type of lonely madness. Not even Kate could rescue me. She wasn't my mother, though I fantasized at night sometimes that she was. But I had to be my own mother and I was horrible at the job.

Even hanging out with Jasmine had become strained because I would not eat. She tried to talk about it. "You're not getting enough calories," she said one night after we hopped a Greyhound bus.

We rode to Niagara Falls, thinking we could find people to party with — adults, people more exciting than our peers. Her mother worked in the hospital as a nurse all night and wouldn't know Jasmine had taken off, and I had no one to report to. We disappeared for the night, and the plan was to take the morning bus back to school, with a great story to tell. On the bus to Niagara Falls, we listened to Prince and shared the earphones to my Walkman, and spoke of our lives in half sentences.

"That guy is bugging me about prostitution," Jasmine said, as if it were the first time I had heard of such things.

"My friend Steff is a prostitute. Don't do it, Jasmine. You don't have to do that," I said.

She was tapping the window from her seat on the mostly empty bus. "He tries to touch me."

"Did you tell your mother?" I asked.

"No. She works so hard on the night shift for me, so I can go to school. I don't want her to feel bad."

I didn't know what to say, not because I was shocked, but because I had heard it so many times before, because I knew what it was like. We stopped talking after we had shared a few of our secrets. It was dark when we arrived in Niagara. The streets were deserted, and we were left at a bus depot without any money and far from anything with lights or action, lost. We found a park and stayed there all night, trying not to get harassed or jumped. Our adventure was dull, anticlimactic, and it was the last time I would spend intimate time with Jasmine.

We drifted apart after that night. She pulled away from me, and I didn't fight it. It was as if we had shared too much, knew too much about each other and it wasn't safe somehow. We were not like the rest, the ones who had driveways and cars at home, Sunday dinners, and parents who bought them Nintendo toys or gave them allowances. I rolled hash oil–covered joints with wild mushrooms and cocaine with young adults I barely knew from grade thirteen. I blotted out for hours on end, no one the wiser but me, and I was a disaster.

I didn't even want friends. They were unpredictable, unreliable teens inside their cookie-cutter lives, while I lived outside of it, looking in. The world was no oyster; there was no pearl inside, just the sounds of my empty stomach in a shallow wasteland of a city. My body was hungry, my brain deprived. I didn't want to read Shakespeare or give book reports. I didn't want to learn fractions or complicated mathematical equations from a boring man who looked as frail as the dying.

"It's not just math, it's how we solve problems in our everyday lives, it's a foundation," our pale math and science teacher said after I refused to try to answer a problem on the board. I thought he was a simple man, someone who couldn't possibly understand my life. He was predictable and ate the same sandwich every day with some vegetables, tea, and crackers. There were no math problems that could solve the killing of animals or the bruised bodies of my sisters. No math that I could relate to. So instead I raged. The teachers didn't understand that my anger was for my parents, not for them.

"You don't know what the heck you're talking about," I blurted out. I tried not to be belligerent, but I just couldn't stop myself. I was angry with any adult who patronized or preached about the building blocks of life and the purpose of things like fractions or pi. "When you figure out how to stop a man from raping a boy, maybe I'll believe that math is the foundation for life," I said, thinking of Steffin and packing up my books. I didn't get very far before I ended up with another detention.

I sat with Anna from grade thirteen. She wore very low-cut tops so she could expose the red rose tattoo above her breast. "Do you like it?" she asked as she slowly revealed more of it by pulling down her bra. She had long black hair and albino-white skin.

I stared at her breast. "Yes, I love it. It's beautiful," I said.

She came closer and passed me her phone number, said I should come out some time and hang out. She was high, I could tell. I couldn't stop staring at her rose tattoo.

I also despised my drama teacher. I thought her lessons were clueless: improv and stretches and boring plays or monologues that were meant to be "safe" material for teens. I thought it was utter bullshit. "What do you know about acting, about people? Why are you even teaching us with this crap? This isn't Disney. We aren't ten-year-olds." I felt horrible, but did not know how to stop the anger from spilling out. I was so wrapped up in my pain that I didn't see my teachers as human: people with bills and families and troubles of their own. I was too young — too damaged — to have compassion, but I was old enough to understand they would not help me. They could not. "This play is shit!" I said just before I was thrown out of class. More detentions. Ms. Kate told me I needed to treat the drama teacher with respect, even if I didn't like what I was doing.

Eventually, I believed that school was just a waste of time. It was tedious and uninspiring. It depressed me. I had thought that once I'd escaped my mother and my past, once I'd found independence, that somehow all my fantasies and dreams would come true. It was all a lie, all a bunch of false information that we ingested from television shows, news, and school, the fallacy of a better tomorrow. Lies.

There would be nothing better, nothing to look forward to. I knew too much. I believed I knew everything there was to know. I believed that kids like me, from violent or broken homes, couldn't buy in to societal norms. They were lies, imposed concepts — marriage and children, houses, nine-to-five jobs — designed to keep us in line. Lines I had no use for. I lived outside of them. I wanted nothing to do with them. With anything.

I was fifteen and no longer satisfied with just starving. Instead, I wanted to die.

*Die* replaced the old *fatso* jingle. The word looped around inside my head. *Die. Die. Die.*

I took twenty-two uppers and thought that would kill me. I walked into the snow near the Riverdale Farm by the forested area where the trees swayed eerily. I sat in the snow. The drugs churned in my belly; chills crept into my bones. I had no gloves or hat. It hadn't occurred to me that the cold would be uncomfortable. How was I supposed to sleep after taking twenty-two uppers? Stupid. It was quiet. Icicles hung from the branches. I made my way back to my apartment and started to vomit. As the night passed, I kept throwing up, but the vomit turned into blood. I went to St. Mike's Hospital the following morning.

The doctor's face was inches from mine inside the cubicle, a small space divided by green curtains that boxed us in. He was a wiry man in a white coat with a stethoscope dangling from his neck. "Why did you take so many pills?" he asked.

"I didn't mean to." I had a tube in my nose that made it hard to talk. "My friends at the party were taking pills and I just took a bunch, but I didn't know I would get sick, that I took too many."

"You shouldn't give in to peer pressure."

"You're right." I could get away with saying anything. My acting lessons had paid off.

"We're going to keep you until tomorrow. Normally we are supposed to send kids like you to psych, so I don't want to see you here again, okay?"

"Okay."

The sounds of the hospital and the smell of disease and medicine lingered over me. I stared at the fluorescent lights and stained ceiling tiles.

It didn't work. I heard the voice inside my head, my companion. *You can try again.*

I thought of calling someone, but I didn't know who. So instead I had a conversation with myself. *You're okay. I'm here. I can be who you want me to be.*

*I want ... I want ... to stay.*

*Here? You want to stay in the hospital?*

*No. Here.*

*You mean the larger here? What for? No one cares.*

*You do.*

*Did you think it would be like this?*

I stared at the flickering light above my head. I hadn't disassociated entirely, was just lonely, and this was my new form of self-comfort, speaking with the voice inside. I needed a friend and it seemed an ingenious way to fill the emptiness.

*No. I figured I would tap my way into the hearts of North America, triple-time step with Sammy Davis Junior, or that I'd be a great scientist, maybe even a great actress,* I answered.

The buzzers went off and I heard someone running. A police officer was in hot pursuit. I heard the screams of the runner as he was cuffed, shouting about the devil and being held in a tiny box.

*Don't leave me,* the voice inside whispered while I held on to myself. *You know we can't stay like this forever.*

*Who says we can't?*

*I don't want to be crazy.*

*No one needs to know. You don't have to talk about me, our secret.*

*But I know.*

*You know I'm you, so you're not crazy.*

I didn't know my purpose, why I was alive. I questioned the importance of being a performer, wondered why I had been born. Was it because I was supposed to be on television or become famous? It just seemed so empty. It wouldn't matter if I died. What would be left behind? Some old TV shows I was in or photographs in a drawer somewhere?

I covered my ears and hummed myself a lullaby, blocking out the sounds and smells and sights of St. Mike's, calmed by the voice inside.

The next morning I promised the doctors I wouldn't do anything harmful and was released. But I kept trying to kill myself — half attempts, full attempts, valium and vodka. I did this a couple of times, intent on killing myself, but each time I would seek help, go to different hospitals. I baited doctors but they did not bite, likely because I lied, expecting that they would discover I was in trouble without my having to tell them. But they didn't know how to connect the dots.

I tried cutting but I was afraid to cut deep enough. Then I thought I would jump into the Don River, hoping to drown, but I was too good a swimmer and knew I would stop myself unless I was weighted down by a rock or bricks or rope, and I was too afraid to try this method.

I opened the oven door and wondered what it would be like to die like Sylvia Plath. I tried: I turned on the heat but immediately stopped because it was so hot! I didn't understand how it worked, except that I might burn and who wanted that? Then I learned that it was supposed to be a gas stove, not electric.

I was not successful in the art of dying, but I was gaining a macabre resumé, practising for what I thought was to come. No one who knew me was aware of these attempts; they were mostly secretive, until I needed medical attention, but even then I was not truly seen. It was obvious I was a teen in need of care, but no one stepped in.

Though I wasn't yet sixteen, I felt like an eighty-year-old. I took seven ludes, sat in a small park near the Bloor Viaduct, and pulled the wrapper off a Skor chocolate bar for my last meal.

I was going to die.

The sky was beautiful, blue and pink under the setting sun. The ludes slowed me down, made me tippy, like a buoy in the ocean. I held on to the cement rail and walked to the centre of the bridge. It was dark out when I looked over the ledge of the viaduct. I saw the headlights of passing cars below. I would certainly die on impact. I imagined the fall, hitting the concrete, how a car would roll over my body. I looked for the best spot to jump from, maybe stalling, maybe not.

I crawled onto the ledge slowly and dangled, with one leg and arm hanging over the edge and one arm and leg hanging over the sidewalk on the bridge, draped over cement like a piece of cloth on a clothesline. It would be as close to instant death as could be, but I was afraid to fall, afraid to die. I went limp and stared at the passing cars flickering like strobe lights below in the night.

I was ripped from the ledge and hit the sidewalk. A woman cradled me on the pavement.

"It's okay," she said. "You're okay." She continued to rock me in her arms while cars passed us on the bridge. Eventually, she lifted me up so we could walk toward the pay phone. I gave her Kate's phone number, as she was the only person I could think of for my strange saviour to call.

I smacked my lips in thirst while the woman spoke to me: "Don't fall asleep. Open your eyes."

"Thank you," I heard Kate say to my bicycle-riding saviour.

"Come on, stand up, Joanne." I felt Kate's leg touching mine, a gentle prod. She reached down to help me up. Her husband, Lionel, was behind the wheel, ready to take us to their home.

She made me eat a bagel in the morning before I washed my hair. I was lying over the edge of the tub with my head under the tap. I didn't want to take a shower. I heard Kate say, "Joanne, the water is running. Do you need me to help you?"

"No." I lifted my head. I heard Kate and Lionel giggling, and I laughed along with them at myself for a second. I wanted them to adopt me; I wanted to tell them I loved them, would be a good daughter, do my homework, and shower properly. My love fell out of me easily. A warm touch, a place to sleep — it didn't take much for me to want, to wish again. The drain swallowed my thoughts as I fell forward, the water took the moment, and I couldn't remember anything, just the slow fog of drugs inside, stealing my memories.

For days I was in a hazy, stoned blur, barely able to keep my eyes open. I slept at Kate and Lionel's place for three days and they forced me to go to school. My science teacher kicked me out of class after I told him to fuck off. I didn't want to study dead things, wasn't interested in the guts of a frog or slicing it open. The only death I was interested in was my own.

I wasn't dead, *wasn't dead*, so I kept trying to lose weight, trying to become so thin I would drop. I hated fat and thought weight loss would eventually kill me. I would die thin and escape this shell I was stuck in. But it was hard to be hungry and ignore my body's signals. I tried to master new regimes: eating one apple with cheese for dinner, then exercising. I drank black coffee with no milk or sugar because of the calories. I allowed myself to eat a muffin with butter at lunchtime. Then I held the butter and just ate the muffin, then I ate only the top of the muffin and left the other half in the wrapper. Then I wouldn't eat anything at all in the afternoon.

Mind over matter.

I pretended to eat, believed I could go without food and feel full. If I fantasized when I had cravings, I could control the desire to eat. My body was screaming for protein, fibre, vitamins, but I would mime the act of eating with my invisible fork, knife, and mouthful of air.

The tiniest amount of flesh looked like hundreds of pounds of fat; there was no distinction. Soon enough my apple-and-sliced-cheese dinner became half an apple. Then I stopped eating dinner altogether, because I was "fat." I could not sleep. I was too hungry for sleep, but I would not eat, so I exercised at midnight, 3:00 a.m., 4:00 a.m., any time of day.

I woke up frantically after I dreamed about food one evening. I felt for the bones in my chest, bounced out of bed to turn on the light, and stood in front of the mirror. I removed my T-shirt and felt my ribs, each curve and indent around my bones. My ribs were like the bars of a prison cell, with my organs threatening to escape. I didn't know that bones could feel so fragile and solid all at the same time, that bones could poke out so awkwardly. They exposed my state of mind without my having to speak.

I pinched my belly and the skin between my fingers and cried because the skin felt like fat and I didn't know the difference between the two anymore. I fell to the ground and felt the cold, hard surface beneath my body; everything was so cold all the time. My fingers were frozen like ice cubes and I rubbed them up and down my legs, tried to warm them.

I was so hungry. I wanted to eat. *No. Get up, move. Get up*, said the voice inside. I sat on the ground to do sit-ups, but my spine hurt from pushing bone against the hard floor, so I did push-ups instead, but couldn't hold myself up anymore and fell to the floor, panting, the air moving quickly in and out of my lungs, my chest heaving, fingers constantly moving over the bones of my body, and all I heard was the voice inside my head, like a direct link from God.

*Just keep moving. Don't tell. Don't talk.*

I wondered if maybe the voice inside was God, thought maybe God was in me.

"If you stand sideways we can't see you anymore, Joanne," people said. I thought they were lying, believed others thought I was fat. Why would I have thought otherwise? It was the message given to me since the age of twelve, and it would take more than a few concerned stares to reverse that message.

My internal organs shook and trembled, like an arm losing circulation, with the sensation of hundreds of needles sticking inside of me. Organs tingled beneath bone and under skin, vibrating. I was terrified, didn't know what to do, didn't know why I hadn't had a period in over a year, or why everything hurt.

I was in the washroom rinsing my hands in the sink, rubbing them dry against my jeans. I started to brush out my long hair when I noticed a clump of hair in the brush. I held my breath and leaned into the mirror, separated strands of hair with my fingers, exposing my scalp where a tiny bald patch became visible. I covered it up by brushing through my hair with my fingers and tying it back into a ponytail. I left the washroom to go to the fridge and pulled out some strawberries and sliced four of them up to eat. I hoped it would stop my hair from falling out. I was hungry and opened the cupboard and found Barry's jar of peanut butter and shoved my fingers into the thick nutty tar, then licked them like a child licks the cake batter from a spoon.

I needed the energy. I was about to do a play with the Montreal troupe. We were touring across the country, starting at the Adelaide Court in Toronto. It was an original musical about teenagers, racism, pregnancy, and abortion. I was playing the part of a girl having an abortion. I would imagine aborting my childhood with the scream on stage that filled the audience while a coffin was paraded behind me. Oh, the symbolism.

# CHAPTER SIXTEEN

THERE WAS A REHEARSAL in Montreal. I took the overnight train and slept in a tiny cabin the size of a closet. A tiny Murphy bed fell over the toilet and took up the entire cabin space. With a window beside me, the chugging sound of the locomotive and the constant motion lulled me into the best sleep I'd had in months. The whistles woke me before my stop and I was picked up at the station by Martha. She was taking me to the apartment I had lived in not that long ago. I wasn't sure how I felt about going back home, but was excited to see my old friends, to hold Steffin, and to run around my old stomping grounds, as if I could, as if my time away had not changed anything and I could slip into Montreal like slipping into old clothes. But when I saw the blood stain on the wall of our old apartment and my mother sitting at the table looking nervous in the kitchen, I knew it would never be the same.

"Why is there blood on the wall?" I asked.

Mother sat at the table with her can of Coke and Martha gestured for me to sit.

"We have something to tell you."

I didn't say anything, just waited.

"Clint was in an accident." Martha looked at me, then at my mother.

"What? Is he okay? What does this have to do with ... is that why there's blood on the wall?" I waited for an answer but none came quickly enough. "Tell me! Is he okay?"

"Yes," my mother finally said. She didn't have much to add, mostly let Martha do the talking.

"Why is there blood on the wall?"

Martha and my mother looked to each other before Martha continued. "He was at a party last night, he got drunk and came over. He was angry, screaming at your mother and wasn't making a lot of sense."

"He cut himself on a beer bottle in the bathroom and he dragged his hand across the wall before he left," my mother piped in. "He was gone before I knew what to do. He was driving his mother's car...."

I tried to absorb the information. Didn't know how to assimilate it, but then it dawned on me that he could be severely injured or dead. "Is he going to make it?" I looked to Martha for some reason, not my mother. I did not want to cry. I tried to hold myself in as tightly as I could.

"He's in a coma."

"I should go see him —"

"That's probably not a good idea," Martha said, looking from my mother to me.

"Why not?" I asked.

"He should be left alone with his family right now," my mother said, sitting with her hands tucked under her breasts like she always did, crossed arms high on her belly. It was odd, the moments remembered — blood on the wall, how my mother sat, the looks between Martha and my mother as if something was missing.

I nodded in acceptance that I would not see Clint. But I didn't know if he would make it, only that I might not ever see him again.

"Tell me what happened," I asked.

Martha filled in the rest of the story, that Clint had hopped into his mother's car, had driven the steep roads of Mount Royal, and was speeding down the hill at a very dangerous corner and smashed into a lamppost head-on. His face hit the steering wheel and his nose was broken and his face cut open, and he was in a coma.

That weekend was a blur. I rehearsed and met friends in a bar, but all I wanted to do was go back to Toronto, get away from my mother. If I couldn't see Clint, I just wanted to go home. I travelled back on the Sunday night train, and tried to forget. I learned soon after that Clint had made it. He woke from the coma. I let it go, let it recede into the back of my mind, and closed the vault. I could move on to my empty fridge, empty stomach, and the end of my first year in the arts program.

I sat with Kate in her office on the last day of school. She wanted to give me her new phone number in case I needed it.

"Take care of yourself. I know you have it in you," Kate said.

"I'm sorry. Sorry if I was too difficult...." I said.

"Why are you sorry, silly? You keep strong. It's not all bad, you know, living. There is so much to enjoy. It's not all tears and drama. The world is big."

I smiled and thanked her for being so good to me, said I was grateful, that I would miss her. All the right words came out. I often fantasized at night that she was my mother and Lionel was my father. Sometimes it helped me fall asleep, kept me alive in a tiny way she just didn't know. I memorized everything about her before the end of that day — the silver necklace she wore, her burgundy shirt. I memorized the warmth in her eyes and drank it up with my last sip of tea before goodbye.

"My number." Kate pulled out a piece of paper from her notepad. I folded it over and over, then shoved it deep into my jeans pocket, protected by the fist I kept clenched around it.

The kick-off to our cross-Canada tour arrived a few short days after my goodbye to Kate. I would miss her, but I would see my old friends from Montreal again. They arrived in Toronto on a Greyhound bus. We were all insanely excited, rehearsing our play about growing up, love, the end of childhood — all reflections of our actual lives packaged inside our play. After a few days of intensive rehearsal, we had our Toronto debut, then left on the tour bus, driving west through Ontario and continuing on all the way to Yellowknife and Whitehorse, not far from the Alaskan border. Then we'd head back east into British Columbia, over to Edmonton, and all the way across to Halifax and Prince Edward Island. The youngest actor in the show was eight years old, and the oldest eighteen.

I turned sixteen the day the bus left. The first thing Steffin had said after we embraced was "We gotta get you laid for your sixteenth, okay?" He looked the same, except he had dyed his long, stringy hair white since I'd last seen him.

Steffin could not get me to eat, no one could, but I made sure that the children ate. I volunteered to pack lunches for the kids, making sandwiches filled with proteins and vegetables, wrapping each one in foil and plastic, brown-bagging them with cookies and fruit — an obsessive need to make sure everyone else was nurtured.

"They don't make size zero, Jo. You're gonna have to eat so you can buy clothes that fit," Steff said. I needed a new outfit for the show. I wanted to wear only sweats and baggy shirts offstage, but I tried some jeans on. Size 2 was on the rack, but nothing smaller. I liked the baggy size 2 jeans, though, and cut a hole with a knife in a leather belt to keep them up.

In Whitehorse, while all the other children slept, I walked along barren roads with the sun still up at midnight, surrounded by mountains. I hoped I might run into a herd of wild horses or ghosts — I figured I might see them better in a place like Whitehorse. The sun illuminated that small corner of the Earth in the middle of the night, but when I did sleep, all I heard in my slumber was the sound of that controlling, anorexic inner voice putting me down until all I felt was enormous pain in my abdomen. I rubbed my belly and tried to breathe and move my feet, as if I could will the pain away from my stomach.

I was starving. *Don't*, the voice inside my head rattled. *Don't*, just like my mother used to say with that wagging index finger. I didn't need anyone to do that anymore; the voice of anorexia was the perfect master, had learned all the lessons of all those who tried to manipulate and shape my body. But the voice in my head was ruthless. I was in a duel with myself, waiting to fall on my own sword.

By the time we arrived in Edmonton, my size 2 jeans were baggier and all of my humour had disappeared along with what was left of my body mass. I was mostly a shell, a ghost of my former self.

I walked along a road in Edmonton as Steffin shouted my name. He caught up to me, a can of Tab in his hand — he drank it like water thinking it would make him slim. We walked while the other kids were at the West Edmonton Mall sitting inside the Burt Reynolds train café or whirling on rides. Steffin and I didn't care much for kid stuff. We were too jaded from drugs, child prostitution, and starvation. We were quite the pair.

"You don't have to scream, I'm right here," I said, even though I was ten paces ahead of him.

"Why do you do that?"

"Do what?" I asked.

"Act like you're the queen of the Earth, like you're the only one with problems."

I turned and stared at him, waited for him to catch up, then smacked the Tab right out of his hand, hitting him in the face with all my might. I was strong for a bag of bones.

Steffin slapped me back and we fought until we stopped and held on to each other, giggling.

"I'm sorry. I didn't mean to hit you so hard," I said, hitting him again.

"Jesus, what the fuck is wrong with you?" We sat on the pavement in the blazing sun and shielded our eyes from the light like two little vampires.

"I can't talk about it, Steffiny." I held my hands up over my brow to look at him.

"I don't want to watch you die," he said.

He tried to connect with me but my brain was starved, damaged, and I couldn't be reached.

"I can't watch you do this —"

"Well, who said you had to watch anything?" I asked.

"Fuck, you're just such a fucking pain in the ass."

"Well, I had to watch while disgusting old men sat there and you sucked their dicks. How is what I'm doing less fucked than that?"

"You're a bitch, you know. Starving has turned you into an A-class bitch."

"Well, fuck off then, Steff." I didn't really want him to, but anorexia was in charge, not me.

"I don't … I don't want to fuck off. I want you to be Joanne again!"

"I'm not her anymore," I said, standing. "Now why don't you go play on the fucking Tilt-A-Whirl and eat shitty cotton candy with everyone else and just leave me alone."

He stood and faced me, saying he would leave me alone if that was what I wanted. We stared at each other and then walked in opposite directions until I yelled that it was indeed what I wanted. "Fuck off," I heard him say before his voice disappeared as we walked farther away from each other.

I wanted to run after him. He was swaying, wearing flip-flops that flicked against his heels and squeaked, his jeans rolled up and his furry legs exposed, his long hair blowing around in the wind. How could you not love him?

I hadn't felt much of anything, but the idea of losing Steffin made me ache. He was part of me somehow, part of my essence in a way. He was closer to me than anyone. We understood each other's lives deeply, like parts of an atom or a cell.

I saw him walking in the distance and wanted to tell him, wanted to tell him the truth, and spoke out loud hoping he might hear, told him that being hungry didn't feel good, that I had a hard time breathing, that it felt like a bone might break, or that I would die before I was ready. But he couldn't hear me.

I kicked the dirt and rocks and walked along the road that seemed utterly isolated, without people or animals or cars, and wiped my eyes dry.

My bones threatened to poke through flesh as my muscles weakened and my body slowly attacked itself, breaking down. I wouldn't drink water anymore because water fed my cells, which meant it was feeding my body, cells multiplying, feeding, growing, making me fat. Surely water would make me fat. Water: two hundred calories.

I tried to understand why water was bad and believed that water had cells that travelled into the body, feeding blood and organs. I was confused, talked to myself about water out loud, words evaporating from my brain like the water I was afraid to drink. I picked at my skin and decided to allow myself to drink coffee. Coffee would give me enough energy to do my play.

No matter what the mode of transportation we took from one city to the next, I would stay standing, with the earphones from my Walkman in my ears, grooving from Toronto to Yellowknife, upright for hours on end while everyone else sat like normal travellers, eating their sandwiches. I crashed around like lightning in the aisles of trains, buses, and airplanes, even when I had not an ounce of energy and it took everything in me to stay standing. And while other young people were touring shops and museums on our days off, I was looking for local cemeteries, visiting graves everywhere we went to talk to the dead. I would starve myself to death. I had finally figured out how to die. I would do this great play, tour the country, and die by the end of the journey.

Only it didn't work out that way.

I was so hungry, I broke down. I purchased a package of Oreo cookies in Edmonton and found an alley. I didn't want to eat in front of anyone; the act of eating was shameful. People stared if I didn't eat, and I believed they would stare if I did. One set of eyes felt like thousands judging me for something they did so easily, without worry or care. Food was intimate.

I pulled a cookie out of the package, smelled and inspected it, then licked it slowly until the wafers started to soften. I bit into it as the sugar melted in my mouth. I finished one cookie, then ate a second one, then a third, and fourth, then stopped and inspected the area to make sure no one was around. I left the bag of cookies on the ground like a bomb in a knapsack.

It wasn't long before the anorexic voice inside my head was yelling at me. The cookies felt like lead in my belly, weighing me down. I panicked and found a local drug store, browsed the stomach section where laxatives, pills, and liquids lined the shelves. I looked at the labels and found a small bottle of ipecac. It was for accidental ingestion of poison. Food was poison. Perfect.

I bought the ipecac and swallowed the thick liquid that tasted like cough syrup. Retching, holding my stomach, I couldn't get up. I ingested the ipecac two hours before the curtain was supposed to rise; it was an antidote to carcinogens, a self-punishment, penance, purging. Giving in to hunger was a sign of weakness, of failure.

# CHAPTER
# SEVENTEEN

"I'M NOT GOING to the hospital." I lay on a couch in a room in the belly of the theatre, in the basement beneath the stage, a plastic bowl on the floor beside me. "I'll be fine," I said to a few people standing over me. I heard the kids warming up above me, their voices hollow echoes.

"You have to go to the hospital," a woman said. She was one of the mothers touring with us. There was an understudy ready to take my place.

I couldn't let that happen; it would destroy my plan. I had to go on stage and I had to starve, those were the two daily rules. Without them I crumbled.

"The cab is here and you have to go to hospital. We will have to carry you out if you don't get up and walk," the mother said.

Normally I liked her. She had her big hair in a bun and wore a floral dress. She was a soft-spoken woman, so generous with all the kids, but at that moment I hated her.

I refused to stand; then the struggle began. One person tried to lift me and I kicked and pushed, then two people grabbed me, then three, then four. In a flash I saw Steffin out of the corner of my eye, standing in the background, mouth open, while I kicked and screamed. A stick figure kicking and fighting so hard I had to be restrained by four people, even though I was half the size of any one of them. They finally got me into the cab.

At the hospital, I was hallucinating. Dehydrated. Colours turned bright inside my head — violet, blue, turquoise, red, yellow — swirling under my lids and bleeding out into the room. Colours everywhere. Sound crashed around me and I drifted back in my mind. I flinched. Someone was in the room. They grabbed my arm and I felt like I was back in my house, like I was eight, and I felt my father's fists and kicks and I was filled with the terror. The nurse stuck me with a needle while the colours in my head mixed with the memory of my mother, naked, rubbing. She was too close. And my father was screaming, calling me a bitch, a whore, and he was so big, and I couldn't run. I couldn't stop him.

Red, purple, blue, all started to bleed into each other, turning turquoise and orange; electrified white shone like a glistening aura. I floated up and out into the colour itself, mystical and beautiful. I was released from the body that kept me trapped. I was evaporating like particles that fly unseen in the air, like water drops and the full spectrum of the rainbow, a mist no longer bound by form.

Then I heard her speak, the nurse. "Come back. Open your eyes, Joanne," she said. "Come back."

The colours faded and the bright blues turned into flat grey, then the white of the hospital room came into focus and I saw the IV, *drip, drip, drip*, stuck to my wrist. I wanted to rip it out but people were watching as the liquid calories were forced into me. A sound deep in my belly rose to my throat, but stuck there. No sound. Just wide-open mouth. Internally I cursed them for bringing me back, for the trap. *Drip, drip, drip.*

*Post-traumatic stress, anorexia nervosa, suicidal*, the voice in my head said.. These were the names of illnesses that could get me locked up. I was warned that I would be institutionalized. *Be careful what you say, Joanne*, said the voice inside. And I was careful.

"Yes, I know what I've done is foolish. I'll never do it again." I was stuck in a small room with a psychiatrist who wore a white coat. He had a moustache, pad, and pen. He stared right into my eyes when he spoke to me, without expression. I crossed my legs and tried to act like a grown-up.

"You're very sophisticated for a sixteen-year-old," he said.

"Yes, I guess I am. I've been living on my own for a while now, you see." I thought I was doing a great job at imitating an adult and continued to tell him I wouldn't repeat my actions.

"Will you stop starving yourself? If you don't stop, you could end up in the hospital for a long while," he said, clicking his pen on the desk.

I stared at his thick grey and brown moustache. I was smoking — strange as it seems now, you could smoke in hospitals then. I inhaled deeply, then delicately flicked the ashes into the ashtray with as much sophistication as I could muster, again crossing my legs, my bony left knee jabbing into the underside of my right leg. "Why doesn't someone help the children who want to eat?" I asked. "There are children dying in Africa that have no food. Why don't you help them?"

"Well, there isn't anything I can do about the children halfway around the world, but I can do something to help you," he said.

*No*, I thought. *My father killed kittens with a shovel, killed them right in front of me and my sister Lou. Can you make that memory go away? And what about my mother? Should I tell you about her? Can you fix me?*

I couldn't say anything I was thinking. I could not say what was at the brim, my jaw clenched. I didn't know how to speak. I didn't know what he would believe. *How ... do ... I ... speak ... words?*

How can you say what you know? *I have no home. I am not loved.*

"I promise to eat, honest I will."

Those were the words I chose. I had to lie.

"You are going to be monitored. If you don't eat we may have to keep you. We've spoken to your mother —"

*Bitch.* I stabbed my cigarette out in the glass ashtray on his thick wood desk. I couldn't get away from her, not even in Edmonton. I had done it, after all that time of being less than perfect, five, ten, fifteen pounds too big, I had lost it and ended up alone in a room, begging for my freedom from a stranger while my mother feigned concern for me, the daughter she once called fat. It was her, and Martha, and Sylvia's measuring tape, and the men who eyeballed my body, instructing me to lose five pounds. Losing all that weight felt like losing them, too, along with their judgments and insults. Gaining weight meant putting it all back onto my bones, each horrible word and roaming eye, and my memories of childhood, lodged inside each pound. That girl was gone and they wanted me to bring her back to life after working so hard to kill her.

My mother could go fuck herself, that's what I thought.

"I'll eat. I want to finish my play, so I have to get out of here. I'll eat, really I will," I said as I bounced my crossed leg up and down.

"Your mother is the main decision-maker here. I'm here to assess —"

"She doesn't get to make the decisions."

"By law she does, as your mother."

"I'm my mother. Me! I take care of me, see?"

I was eventually released.

The mother who made me go to hospital sat with me in the cafeteria. It had round plastic-covered tables and circular orange benches, with bright fluorescent lights above. The place was filled with hungry people who ate and spoke with frenetic energy, but it was not as oppressive as the rotting smell of unrecognizable

processed meats in the air, or the dull green beans and mashed potatoes smothered in fat that sat in large steel food warmers under the
spotlights of the hospital buffet. Starving was far more appealing.

A tray of food sat in front of me holding toast, juice, and an
egg. I wanted to gag. The mother stared at me and waited. After
taking a bite of the hardboiled egg, I chewed and chewed, feeling
like a trapped feral cat, and tried not to panic. I did not want to
swallow the egg and shoved the mushy mess into the pockets of my
cheeks and under my tongue.

"Can I go to the washroom? I have to pee," I said.

"You didn't swallow. Please finish. If you don't eat you can't do
the show, and you'll have to go back to the hospital. You can do it."

She wasn't mean, she was nice really, but she didn't understand
what she was asking me to do. They were taking away the only thing
I had: control over what I put into my body. But I had no choice.
If I didn't want to sleep in a mental institution, then I had to eat.

So I swallowed the egg.

# CHAPTER EIGHTEEN

"YOUR MOTHER CALLED and said she hasn't been able to reach you and wondered if you were okay," Kate said. I was back at school, uncomfortable in my skin and the size of my body after being forced to eat. My death-wish summer had ended without my death.

Looking down at my hands was a habit I adopted while starving, trying to see the bones in my wrists and the veins popping out from the top of my hands. I didn't realize I had completely gone silent. "What?" I asked.

"You must check in with your mother. You can use the pay phone in the hallway."

Kate could get me to do anything — homework, help other students, clean up. Sometimes she ate with me, watched my intake, but she never forced anything. And she always made me think when she spoke. She knew some of my views, which included not eating as an act of solidarity with starving children in other countries, kids who could be fed if wealthy countries cared enough to provide food. "Dieting is a luxury," she said. "Girls starve themselves into stupidity while others have no choice but to starve. If you really want to help kids in other countries, well, they don't need your martyrdom. Get well, get healthy, and then go do some good, yeah?"

It was impossible to argue or match Kate's reasoning with an equal comeback. She flipped that do-gooder thought right on its head. I wasn't certain that most people would call anorexia a do-gooder deed, but while starving I was able to convince myself of anything. And why would others care if I starved myself in protest? They didn't even know; no one did. Not even Kate understood my childlike reasoning, the personal hunger strike of an anorexic girl. It was private, solitary, with no picket sign, no media scrum, nothing that said *Starving in protest of child abuse around the world.*

Shuffling down the carpeted hall, chewing the skin around my fingernails, I wondered what to say to my mother. I thought of the rivers Ms. Kate taught me about, how they moved from the largest of them all, the Nile, across continents and countries, Africa to Egypt, to the Rio Grande on the Gulf of Mexico, to the St. Lawrence River, place of my birth in Quebec, to the fast-moving waters in me, of blood and salt, liquid, my legs, building strength with each step.

"Will you accept the charges?" the operator asked.

"Joanne? Joanne, are you there? I'm worried. I haven't been able to get a hold of you," Mother said in a higher pitch than her regular tone. It felt fake and made my throat constrict. There was a catch; there had to be a reason for the so-called worry. "What's wrong?" she asked.

I gathered my courage. "I don't want to talk to you. I don't want you to call me or look for me. I just want you to leave me alone. Oh ... and you're fired. You are no longer my manager." My lips quivered as heat catapulted from my belly to my face with each word that flew out of my mouth.

"Joanne, you can't just fire me, I'm your mother." She spoke in that patronizing tone. "That eating problem has changed you, and you're not thinking —"

"Stop it. I'm firing you as my manager. You don't get to make money off me anymore." She'd kept the money I'd earned from *Sesame Street*, my first movie, and the television shows I had done while living at home.

"Who do you think you are, speaking to me in that tone? Don't you think I've paid enough for you to go to that school —"

"Fuck off!" I slammed the receiver down.

Ms. Kate stood at the opposite end of the hallway. We smiled at each other before she instructed me to get back to class. I was fairly certain she'd overheard my conversation, but couldn't be sure; I only know that there was a silent nod on both our parts before I ran to class.

My mother left messages on my answering machine. "You want to be on your own and not talk to me, then you can pay your own way and see how far you make it without my help."

I would make it, no matter what I had to do. There would be no turning back. If parenting was about finances, then I would parent myself. She'd already abandoned the other parenting duties.

She needed to be needed. Every time my mother got rid of another child, it seemed she wanted us to crawl back: "See how far you get without my help." As if she knew we would not survive without her, or could not, that she had bred dependent daughters who would not make it in the world without her directives or control. It was hard to build ourselves up with a mother who undermined her children's development, when she tried to knock us down. And while she berated and belittled us, she built herself up, became more powerful, false or not. There was one place in the world where she would always be needed and have power. But I wouldn't allow myself to need her and I would never call her. That was my resolve, to be motherless.

Then the phone messages changed to "I miss you" and "I love you."

Hearing those words made me cringe, when she said she loved me. I didn't believe it. It felt like she was screaming "Love me, care for me, I need you." *I love you* was loaded.

I needed a good agent at a reputable agency. I found the actor's union and a list of agents. I had learned a few things from my mother about being a shark.

There was no money in the bank — not even my father's child support made its way into my account — but I refused to contact my mother. I had no desire for school, no time for education. Education was for kids who had parents who packed lunches in backpacks; education was a child's luxury I could not afford. So I auditioned for television shows and movies. Sometimes there just wasn't any money and I took whatever jobs I could find — at a corner store, at a bar in the entertainment district as a busgirl. I was still too young to serve liquor and couldn't waitress. Then there were television gigs, the jobs that mattered: being cast as the guest star on TV shows like *Street Legal*, *Night Heat*, and even one starring Mr. T, in which I played a teenage mother with a baby on my hip and a bruised face. I was paying the rent.

There was a Mac's Milk on Yonge Street where I worked the midnight to 8:00 a.m. shift with two drag queens. The St. Charles Tavern was up the block and numerous customers came in at all hours of the night, scanning the store for soda, chips, smokes, or groceries. Some were high, some threatening. Some were young, gay male prostitutes. The St. Charles was also a hotspot for drugs.

"You keep your pretty little ass out of that place, you hear me, girl? You'll end up with a pimp and a case of crabs before too long," one of my co-workers said. He wore a long wig, lipstick, tight jeans, and heels. My other co-worker would arrive dressed in drag on occasion after singing at the club in the gay village and would change into street clothes in the backroom. The owners of the Mac's Milk were two elderly women with soft hearts for young people like the three of us who worked the overnight shift together. I made muffins and pastries at 4:00 a.m., lining muffin tins with premade batter and baking all the sugary foods for the morning crowd, who would come in for coffee and baked goods before work.

One morning, just after I got a batch into the ovens, three young men came in and started taking things from the shelves. My two co-workers dropped to the floor behind the front counter, terrified. I, on the other hand, still had the stupid bark of a belligerent teen. "You put that shit back where you got it," I screamed, jagged as a porcupine.

The three men laughed at me while my co-workers looked up at me with their fingers over their mouths to shush me. I ignored them. When I looked up, one of the men was staring at me from the other side of the counter. He had a baseball cap on and a thick scar on his chin. I tried not to look at it. "I'll take what I want, bitch. What are you gonna do about it?"

I didn't say anything, just felt panic in my bones as he leaned in over the counter to intimidate me, while the two at my feet slunk down on the floor. I stared at the cameras that lined the store. They were on a timer. Every thirty seconds the camera would shift from the front of the store to the back of the store, then back to the front. I knew because I learned to count as I walked the aisles putting food inside my pants: peanut butter, jelly, crackers, bars. By the time the camera came back to the front, I had what I needed to take home. I felt guilt for stealing from the two women who employed me on the overnight shift, but there was never enough money in my pockets. I could steal, but these men could not. There were principles about theft. I looked at the cameras so that they would know they were being filmed. The guy in front of me followed my gaze to the swivelling camera and decided to leave, the others behind him.

"Crazy girl. Next time, you get your ass on the ground beside us, you see a group of men walk through this place. You trying to get us killed?" one of the drag queens said after the guys had left. "I'm calling the manager." He walked to the back of the store followed by our other co-worker.

"Sorry," I said. I knew why there were three of us on the overnight shift. It wasn't safe for one or two. That job didn't last long.

I had gained a lot of weight back in the six months since being hospitalized in Edmonton. It didn't take long for the pounds to return, for the muscles, bones, and organs to rebound. Insecurity settled in along with the weight. Calorie counting was still a habit, and with every mouthful of food I consumed, fewer of my bones were visible. The bones had become friends at my lowest weight. In the bath or lying on my side, feeling my ribs or hipbones had been a comfort, soothing, as if I were embracing someone each time, feeling a familiar bone. But I was losing them. With the returning weight, I buried my friends one by one until I could no longer feel them, and instead, memories took their place, night terrors and memories of the childhood I tried to forget.

I became a pro. People acknowledged my budding career: casting agents, producers, directors. I was the next hopeful, the one to watch for. But I had zero self-esteem, and the inner voice was always there, waiting to tear me down. As an actor, I needed that part of myself to cope with the judgmental and unforgiving film industry, the ones invested in keeping me skinny, subservient, and silent, like an abusive father or husband.

And there were adults who thought it was okay to stick their tongues down my throat, and men who wanted to play strip poker with me in hotel rooms. They thought I was naive, behaved as if they knew my inner world, as if they were the first to show me affection, attention, the first who dared to cross my physical boundaries. But these were the same people who had the power to hire or fire me, the ones I stepped away from, the ones who tried to touch my thighs and get me to take my top off, to show them my body — "for the part."

I was seventeen when an older male director with white hair asked me to take my top off. It was down to two of us for the part after a few auditions. It would be the last callback. The role was a young street girl, a prostitute a middle-aged man would help get off the streets. The room was warm with the camera lights on. The director sat through my audition, then came up to me, walked me to a corner of the room with his arm around my shoulder, and whispered, "Will you take your top off?"

I stiffened, frozen in place. He didn't seem to pick up the cues that I didn't want him holding me, that it was uncomfortable. Or maybe he didn't care to notice.

"I want to see if you can play the part of a prostitute, be uninhibited ... you know."

Oh, I knew, and I was instantly aware that if I said no, I would not get hired and would lose the leading role, not to mention the money. Money I needed to pay the rent. I was close to being that girl in real life, on the streets, uncertain how to make a living. Just like this old man in the audition room, another old man had approached me in the park a few weeks before. He pulled a wad of cash from his pocket and asked if I had seen a girl about my age with red hair. When I said no, he asked me if I wanted to make some money. All I would need to do would be to follow him into the wooded area beside the Riverdale Farm and beat him with his belt by a tree. I hadn't eaten that day, and not out of choice, and only had a nickel in my pocket, which I used to purchase a piece of licorice. My belly rumbled as the old man with wrinkled skin, white hair, and a wad of cash stood above me. I knew he was a predator, but I followed him anyway because I was hungry. So I took his money, and I beat him with the belt, and I ate that day.

But I would not be manipulated by this director. I had my boundaries in my career, or at least I was trying to. I needed someone to rescue me, like the character in the very film I was auditioning for, to swoop in and help me. Instead, I ended up with this guy, arms around me in a corner asking me to take my top off. Irony.

"Will you take your top off so I can see that you can do it?" he asked in a new way.

"No," I said and left the room. *Of course I can take my top off, fucker, but not for you.*

Whoever said one person can make a difference? No one would know if I got fired or how hard I tried behind closed doors to fight for myself and for other girls. It was futile, but I didn't know it, wouldn't know that the struggle would last a very long time for girls and women. But who would fight for me? Who would house me if I couldn't work?

I had been working since the age of eight, and it didn't matter that I had a career, that I was not *actually* a prostitute: unless I took my top off when old men requested, I would be discarded.

# CHAPTER NINETEEN

DRUGS SQUELCHED the rage that had become my normal state of being, so I chased the state of euphoria I found in them, the escape, until I came down, until my skull ached and my limbs hurt. After not receiving the role in the movie, I went on a bender and snorted too much cocaine. I was struggling in the morning when Lou called and woke me up. News was that our mother had disappeared from Montreal, like Houdini, just up and left without telling a soul, not even Lou. She also stole people's money before her silent exit. I put the phone on my bed, a cigarette dangling from the corner of my mouth. I coughed and held the phone receiver in one hand, grabbed the glass of water from the bedside table with the other hand. I wiped my eyes and licked my dry lips, trying to wake up and take it all in.

I had turned seventeen and was renting a room in a house with two other tenants in the east end of Toronto. My room was bare, save for the posters of Madonna, Janis Joplin, and Jimmy Dean. Old cinema ticket stubs sat in jars on my dresser, and my clothes were scattered on the floor. My roommates were all double my age. One woman was always perky; she worked in an office and went to bars at night. Another wore Jane Fonda workout clothes — tights, body suits, and leg warmers — around the house, and had long blond hair, feathered like Farrah Fawcett's in *Charlie's Angels*. She was obsessed with the famous twenty-minute workouts. I was the opposite of those women: a dark-haired, no-makeup-wearing, cigarette-smoking tomboy. The owner of the house seemed obsessed with sex and girls.

I rubbed my legs, hadn't quite woken up, and tucked my long hair behind my ears so it wouldn't fall on the lit cigarette. By the end of our conversation, I had decided to move back to Montreal, to get away from this new rental and go back to my hometown, now that my mother was no longer in it. I would be able to write and direct a play in the company. Martha had always left the door open for me to do that work in her theatre; in fact, she often encouraged me to work with them. And I missed Montreal, the mountain, the French language, missed Steffin and my old friends. It wouldn't take much to move — a van, a few bucks for gas.

Lou lived in an apartment on Saint Laurent Boulevard, which was busy with cars, bars, and partying at all hours of the night. I slept on a futon in the living room, where the sounds of the street drifted in through the windows. It was the type of distraction I needed; it helped me fall asleep, drowned out my thoughts in the middle of the night. The city noise was a sort of bedtime story; I listened to fights between lovers or the drunks trying to find their way home while the street lights flickered on and off.

Montreal was still the place of my birth. It had culture and distinct architecture — the winding wrought-iron exterior stair- cases throughout the city, the narrow cobblestone streets of old Montreal, the solid grey-stone buildings with the river below. But even with the familiar physical landscape and people, something was missing — a sense of belonging. I longed for it, tried to find it with Lou.

Lou spent a lot of time indoors, reading tarot cards for people and giving advice. She had long curly orange hair and big brown freckles that peppered her face. She wore a red nightgown at home or long hippy skirts with flowing shirts and beads, bright-blue eyeshadow, and thick eyeliner. People loved Lou. She had a way of making people feel like she had the answers to their problems or questions, a mystic. Her visitors were like us, teenagers or young adults trying to survive in an adult world.

At night, I walked along the streets crowded with markets and swiped goods from local vendors — pepper, powdered garlic, salt, crackers, chocolates, playing cards, small toys. I wore boyish clothes: black jeans, black leather jacket, T-shirts, and sometimes a fedora. If it weren't for my long hair and girlish face, I would have been mistaken for a guy. I occasionally heard "Excuse me, sir." I didn't much care if people thought I was a boy or a man. I liked it; it made me feel different, less vulnerable, almost myself. And then my heart rate would escalate while I walked by the two lesbian bars on Saint Denis Street, as if even looking at them and pondering about who and what was inside might give away my secret and growing desire. I wanted to go inside. There was no shame in this acknowledgement, only fear. I was afraid of being accosted, afraid of how people might think less of me, but I wasn't ashamed of the feelings, or of my truth. I just hadn't fully realized it or consciously accepted who I was.

"Why would an eighteen-year-old girl want a penis?" Lou asked one night after we had smoked up. I told her I liked being mistaken for a man but I didn't want a penis. I didn't like anything about penises. She didn't seem to care one way or the other, only she did seem confused about the anatomy part, or maybe it was I who was confused.

We drank beer and sat in our rounded orange plastic chairs. They had legs missing, and when we sat in them they swayed and bobbled on the floor like a tipping boat until we could balance them and be still. Our walls held sketches of faceless women, posters of French artists, a man playing the trumpet, and an empty canvas waiting for inspiration. Lou wanted to glue the hair of her dead cat to it.

We had picked up exactly where we'd left off when I was fourteen. From five hundred kilometres away, Lou had still been the person I called in emergencies. And there had been several.

"Stop fucking dying on me," she had screamed numerous times over the phone. "You're always trying to die. If you are going to die, die! Just do it," she said once when I was skin and bone.

I couldn't blame her. Even before our mother disappeared, we had been motherless girls, and while Lou worked hard at not drowning, I was always trying to sink.

Lou had spent her childhood suffocating under our mother's constant comparisons and criticism, and there was little I could do to make up for it.

But in Montreal as roommates we were very different, having grown into different worlds. She practised musical notes and scales on a keyboard, read tarot, and spent days on end in her apartment, while I spent my time writing a play on a vintage typewriter, snorting far too much cocaine, and venturing out alone at night.

I finally mustered my courage and would sneak into the lesbian bars in the dark of night, disappeared inside to watch women dance together, watch how they held each other and smiled so comfortably. I loved to watch them kiss, touch. It all looked so natural, felt right, like something I had been missing. These bars were tucked-away places that I grew to love, my secret nightly excursions. I wanted to be like these lesbians, to hold on to a woman without noticing anyone else around, a woman with curves, breasts, and soft skin. I wanted to be on the dance floor, weaving my limbs like a braid with another, swaying to a slow tune.

Lou noticed the way I was dressing and commented. When we talked, I told her I felt safer dressing like a man. But Lou knew there was more to what was going on with me than my clothes. I was not transgender; just uncomfortable in my skin, my body, and didn't know how to identify. *Lesbian* seemed liked the closest word, only I hadn't come out yet to Lou.

Lou inhaled and rocked from side to side in her orange chair, all colour coordinated from her red hair to her red robe. We shared a joint while Marianne Faithfull's "Broken English" played in the background, and we talked about the streets and the safety of women. The candles flickered and cast shadows on the walls as we talked about the differences between genders. I liked it when it was just the two of us. Lou didn't pretend to have all the answers to life's questions. She may have been otherworldly, but she was just my big sister, the one who had braided my hair when I was little, the one I sang songs and shared bedrooms with.

"I don't want to be a guy, Lou, I just … I don't know what I want, who I am."

I wanted to be invisible to men, didn't want reminders of femininity. There was something about the natural occurrence of a body bleeding without violence that both amazed and terrified me. Having periods was the strongest reminder of my gender, the vulnerability. I just hadn't figured out its power.

Surely the gods had messed that gendered part up. Being a man could change everything, but I didn't really want to be a man because I felt like one; it wasn't that. But how could I be a lesbian and not want to be a woman? What was a woman? How could I want to love women if I didn't want to be inside my own body? I was confused.

"Wanna get some cocaine, Lou?" I changed the subject.

She wanted to know where I would get it and how we could afford it. I didn't say, only that I knew how and where. "Then hell yeah. Get your ass outta' here and bring home the powder!" Lou smiled and rolled sideways, falling out of the rolling orange chair. "I gotta pair of socks you could stuff into the crotch of those jeans of yours ..."

I called and met up with Steffin on Sherbrooke Street outside Les Foufounes Électriques, filled with young people all dressed in black, spikes, leathers, heels, with sex in every corner. I went to the girls' bathroom and met the dealer, Pierre. We squeezed into a tiny stall where he sat on the tank of the toilet with his back against the wall and his feet on the closed seat. We asked him for a loaner on the blow. I stared at the graffiti on the walls — "Frederique loves Denise," with blue ink hearts around it, and "Put your penis through this hole," under which there was a drawing of an open mouth.

Pierre smirked. He had the prettiest long ringleted black hair.

"I've heard this before. What are you going to do for me if you don't pay me on time?" he asked, looking right at me.

"Whatever. If you want a blowjob, I'll give you a blowjob," I said, to see if it would work.

Steffin laughed while Pierre tucked his hair under his beret. A long dark coat, lined with baggies of cocaine, covered his skinny frame. He was handsome, young.

*Bang, bang, bang.* "Anyone in there? Pierre, you there?"

"Please?" I asked.

"Yeah, she's good for it, especially the blowjob part," Steff said.

I looked at Pierre, waiting for an answer.

"Okay. But remember your promise. No money and ..." Pierre grabbed his crotch.

On the way back to Lou's, Steffin and I giggled about blowjobs being *his* domain.

"Would you even know how, Jo?"

"I wouldn't laugh if I were you, cause if we don't pay up, you're going to have to do the honours," I said. But I didn't think about the danger, or how little self-worth we had, or how simple it was to offer my body as collateral for momentary pleasures like drugs. It was what I knew, what I had always known, that my body could be traded, that I was a commodity. It was the largest lesson I had retained from my childhood, and I was still young and brave in all the wrong ways.

Back at the apartment, the Talking Heads blasted through the speakers. I bounced on the wooden floor as if it were trampoline, cocaine high, to "Burning Down the House." Lou and Steffin were in the wobble chairs, singing, with powder on the table and a rolled-up bill sitting on a tiny mirror. Diana Ross came on and we all hopped up in a dancing frenzy. Lou, in her mahogany robe, flailed wildly. Cocaine joy, no inhibitions, just abandon. It went on for hours until not even the city streets were alive with noise. Montreal had fallen asleep when the sun rose, and so had I.

# CHAPTER TWENTY

I WAS WRITING a play on an old green typewriter, a play about child sexual abuse for our youth festival. Young people, ages twelve to eighteen, had come from Vancouver, Amsterdam, even Australia, to be part of our theatrical festival. I typed for hours every day and only took breaks to rehearse with the kids.

The festival was important to me, my link to the city I loved, with the kids, many of whom I had known for years. They were like glue; they helped keep me together somehow. Perhaps it was the familiar, the people who still existed and had not disappeared. I had also become one of the young leaders, directing and casting, and I was responsible for kids younger than me — making sure they were at rehearsals, ate lunch, and had transportation home. There were many kids from Montreal. Some I had seen grow up, like Marc and Geneviève, first loves like Clint and I had been. But they were younger and truly innocent kids who played and danced and sang songs, listening to Kris Kross's "Jump," as they tried out their new breakdance moves.

"Look, Joanne, look at this." Marc smiled while he showed me how to do the wave and the Michael Jackson moonwalk.

Geneviève had a cast on her leg, but sang along as I tried to learn the moves, and they laughed at me after my first attempt at the moonwalk. I let them.

"How are you two love birdies chirping?" I enjoyed watching them squirm with embarrassment. They'd turn red and laugh, the sweetest kids.

I had once, five years before, seen Marc lunge out of the elevator. He was terrified, said a man had followed him into the lobby and tried to touch his private parts. I ran and grabbed a baseball bat from our rehearsal hall and tore out of the building. I couldn't find the pedophile, but I would have done anything for those kids, as if they were my young siblings.

It was okay if they laughed at me when I attempted the moonwalk. They had nothing on me. "Try this," I said as I triple-time stepped, as if my tap shoes were on. A dance-off between Marc and me, with Geneviève watching from her chair, moving her crutches like limbs to the beat. We danced until it was time for rehearsal.

There was also Malcolm, who wore a button-down shirt and often pushed his glasses higher on his nose with one finger while talking. He gave me a copy of the book *Malcolm X* and told me he was a descendant of the civil rights activist. He was a boy trying to find his way, one who wanted to understand everything. "How can people go about their days and not talk about what they did to our people?" he'd ask, or "What is the meaning of peace?" or "What are we all going to do if they drop a nuclear bomb?"

I didn't know who "they" were, only that Malcolm always wanted to talk after rehearsal, that he was an intellectual, full of passion and sadness for a fifteen-year-old. I usually listened, tried to pump up his confidence when I could — as if it might even rub off on me and I might take my own advice. But I rarely did.

These kids were not like I was. They had bedrooms with posters and matching colours. They had parents and braces and went home to meals on the table. They were not sniffing cocaine, or trying to figure out where to live next or if they could afford to buy food that night. I hid as much of myself as I could to be a role model. I tried anyway.

There were many children and teenagers who saw me as a mentor or confidante after so many years in the company. My instinct was to protect them. My role meant I could impact their lives, provide a little hope for others even though I still hadn't learned how to hold on to it myself. Seeing it in the faces of younger kids made it possible, and it provided a deeper purpose other than being a writer, a director, and an actor. I pretended to be mature for the little ones, who would occasionally run up to me for hugs or to tell me about their day or ask for advice. There were even suicidal kids looking for help. I was not qualified, but I did what I could. I could not erase my own pain, but if I could help other kids, it meant healing was possible.

One evening after getting home from the theatre, I planned to sneak out to a lesbian bar, but the doorbell rang. It was Martha, smoking her Rothmans nervously and pivoting about like a busy ant. "I just thought I would check in on you. Tried to catch you after rehearsal today, but you had left already. Wanted to see if we could go for a pitcher of beer. My treat. I need to talk with you," she said with a nervous giggle. It made that old feeling surface, the one that the *We need to talk* phrase always conjured: dread.

"Sure. I could use a drink. Was just about to take off, so good timing."

I grabbed my fedora and leather jacket and put on my black Doc Martens boots before we walked down Saint Laurent to the local pub. It was hard to say no to Martha, but I would have preferred my secret hideaway with the women. I wondered, maybe, if she wanted to ask me about my identity, about being a lesbian. She had asked me when I was twelve if I thought I liked girls and I remember saying no. I'm not certain why she did that. At the time she said she noticed that I hugged her a lot, that I seemed to want to be close to her. I remember the embarrassment and discomfort. I was a kid in search of affection and love, but she confused that with something sexual: an odd choice. I wore ponytails and overalls, carried a plastic animated figurine in my pocket with waxy perfume in it, and rolled around on roller skates. If I was exploring sexuality at that time, it was with other twelve-year-olds, not adults who had authority like my mother, who crossed boundaries because they had none. But maybe she wanted to ask again. Maybe someone had spotted me at a bar and she wanted to tell me she knew. I would say yes if she asked.

The nervous tension that followed us from the apartment to the pub ramped up. I sat in a stained old velvet-padded chair at a small wooden table with green felt coasters on it. Jazz from the radio played in the background. Martha paced on the spot at the bar, her face dotted with concern. Or was it fear? It made my insides twist, but I tried to remain calm while Martha stared at me from the bar. She wore a flower-covered skirt and a grey sweater, the one she wore all the time, that slid off of one shoulder. She always smiled at people flirtatiously and would lift her naked shoulder and suck on her cigarette as if it were something far more suggestive. But now she was staring at me and swaying from side to side, extremely anxious. She grabbed the pitcher of beer and sat down across from me.

"What's wrong?" I asked, unable to cope with that frenetic energy much longer.

Martha poured the beers and drank half a cup before she wiped her mouth with the back of her hand. "Okay, I have to tell you something, something really important, and I'm afraid," she cried. Tears ran down her cheeks, not just a few tears, but streams. We both drank.

"What is it? Why are you crying?"

"I'm so scared you're going to hate me. I can't lose you...."

"You're not going to lose me," I said, tapping my feet under the table, not certain I wanted to hear, but wishing to get it over with — whatever *it* was. She had been my drama teacher, coach, friend. I'd shared my bed with her in Toronto. I knew many of her secrets, the ones she'd confided in me, even when I was only twelve and she was twenty-eight. Adult tales about dates and sex, or her history and family. Even with her lack of boundaries, I had learned a lot from her. I loved her, even if she pushed my buttons or crossed the line sometimes.

"It's about Clint."

"Clint?" I took a large swig of flat beer and then filled my glass up. Martha cried so much it was almost uncomfortable, but in the pub no one really cared.

"It's more about your mother, and Clint, and you." She knew I didn't like to talk about my mother, so whatever it was, it had to be bad. "Remember the night of the accident?"

Of course I remembered. How could I forget? It had been Martha and my mother who sat with me after it happened.

"It wasn't what you thought. And I should have told you sooner. Please forgive me."

"Just tell me."

"Your mother was having an affair with him. I knew and never told you. It wasn't how it seemed ..." Martha confessed. I tried to pay attention but felt like I had just been kicked, like that twisted knot in my gut had ruptured. I didn't want to cry; Martha was crying enough for the two of us. Instead, I drifted, disconnected from my limbs like I did when I had flashbacks, floating away, half there, half not. I tried to stay present, to listen, but I felt like I was suffocating.

"She used to tell me how much she was into him. I told her to leave him alone, that she shouldn't act on it. I mean, she was your mother."

I didn't know what to say. My heart was in my throat.

"I'm sorry. I told her to stop. The night of the accident, he was at a party and kids were spreading rumours about him and your mother, making fun of him. He went to see her, just left the party in a panic. He was drunk. He told her other teenagers knew about them."

The tears fell from her face while she rocked and talked obsessively, without breathing, without any space for me to speak. Even if I could have spoken.

While she talked, I envisioned Clint at our apartment with my mother. I focused on the word *affair*. Affair? Really? My mother? A teenager? That wasn't an affair. I wanted to scream, but all I could do was sit quietly, trying to reorder my reality. I couldn't fathom my mother doing that with Clint. It had never, never occurred to me, at all.

"I wanted to tell you for so long and I know I should have. I don't know why I didn't tell you."

Martha had known my mother was seducing him while I lived there as a thirteen-year-old. She knew and kept it a secret. So it was safe to tell me after my mother had left Montreal? Why now? I wanted to know, but couldn't ask. I couldn't stomach the conversation, calling sexual abuse an affair. Clint was still a minor under the law; more than that, he was my first love. My mother seduced my first boyfriend. I was shocked silent by all the deception.

Clint was cutting himself and trying to tell me without speaking the words; I just didn't know. I didn't recognize it, which was odd because I had done the same things he had — stuffed everything down, raged inappropriately. I tried to tell, too, but I couldn't find the words. There was no way to describe her manipulations. My mother was a master. A trickster. We were just kids. *I'm sorry, Clint.* I just wanted to see him, not listen to Martha.

I stared at her for a while. She stared back.

"There's something else I have to tell you," she said. "Sorry, I just need to go to the washroom first. I'll be right back." She stood up, tucked her chair in, and disappeared.

I took a big sip of beer and rubbed my temples. I didn't think there was much more I could bear. My mind was racing. Was it about Martha, or more about Clint and my mother? I looked around and wanted to run, felt as if everyone were staring at me, which they were not. I got up and walked toward the entrance of the pub and deeply inhaled the outside air before I went back to my seat.

"Hey." Martha had a tissue in her hands. She took a swig of her beer and sat back down.

I said hey back before she carried on.

"I have to tell you. I tried to help when you were younger, tried to listen to your mother, thought it would help if I did," Martha said while I swallowed and my jaw locked. "Your mother told me that she ... she told me that she was sexually attracted to you when you were a little girl. I told her it was sick, but she told me. She also told me how she used to tell your father that you girls had done something wrong, to make him mad, so he would beat you, so she could watch. It excited her!" Martha was crying so hard I thought she might choke, but I couldn't move, had glue in my mouth. My mother was a monster.

"I told her she needed to let you go, to let you leave, live somewhere else. I tried to help," Martha finished.

I said nothing, just stared blankly ahead.

"I'm so sorry. I should have told you. I should have told you sooner and — do you forgive me?" Her eyes were puffy and red from the waves of tears. "Please. I'm sorry. Forgive me." She rocked gently.

"Okay," I said. I could not look at her any longer while she pleaded. I said okay because it was the only way to get away from her pain, because I couldn't breathe. Because I didn't know what else to do in that moment and because I was used to emotionally taking care of her, of adults. I hadn't had any time to process what I had been told, let alone forgive a woman who had deeply betrayed me, who knew such dark secrets, who had colluded with my mother in keeping them for so long.

"Thank you. I'm so sorry. I don't know what I would have done otherwise."

"I have to use the toilet." I got up and rushed to the washroom, bent over the toilet, and wretched.

The rest was a blur, saying goodbye, getting home. Martha had done nothing about the beatings when we were children, about my mother being attracted to me. How could she accept that admission from my mother and do nothing? Telling me then would have been just as useless as telling me at the age of eighteen. Going to the authorities and telling them would have been the right thing to do.

I couldn't make sense of it, only knew that I felt exposed, ashamed. And I felt guilt that my mother had sexually abused Clint, that he nearly died. Part of me thought, in that moment, that it was my fault. I believed I had some ownership or power. If he hadn't been my boyfriend, my mother never would have met him. If I had never brought him home, if I, if I. If. Only.

I tried to piece together different versions of that night until I finally understood what the truth was.

Steffin was one of the culprits. He was at the party where Clint had been before he drove to my mother's apartment. Steffin and the other guys were jeering, taunting Clint with the jingle "Clint's dating Mrs. V." It was child's play, but it wasn't play, and they had set something into motion that could not be taken back. He was already drunk when he hopped into the car and drove to my mother's place in a panic, believing that everyone knew.

Clint told me his version on the phone later, after I gathered my courage and tracked him down by calling all the people with his last name from the phone book until I found him. His voice was tentative yet friendly at first, almost giddy, as if we were teens again. But then I felt her, my mother, as if she were right there with us, as we had always felt that magnetic pull, and while he spoke to me I felt her staring at me, could almost hear her voice in my head trying to stop the conversation we were about to have. But she could not. She had silenced us for so long. He knew why I had tracked him down.

"She used to give me presents and somehow it made up for it," he said with false confidence.

"Made up for what, Clint?"

Then he confirmed everything I had imagined, everything I deep down knew.

"If it had happened in this day and age she would have been put away, called a pedophile. I was a boy. She bought me beer, she fed me, took me out, she gave me money. It was hard to say no, and it's not like your mother was attractive to me. I went to a party that night, and I was upset because some of my friends knew somehow, or thought they knew. They were all saying your mother and I were sleeping together. And I panicked and drove to your mother's place. She wanted me to leave, but I was so drunk I cut myself and tried to get her to drive me home. I told her that my mom needed the car, but she wouldn't drive me. She pushed the car keys into my hand after giving me a mickey of rum while I was there, and I drank the whole thing. You sure you want to know this, Joanne?"

"Yes," I said quietly.

"Okay. She made me leave. She told me I had to go and I did. Maybe your mom didn't want people to know what she was doing to me. I shouldn't have been driving."

I inserted a few apologies between his sentences. As he spoke, it was as if I had been with him in the car, a phantom passenger.

I'd imagined the crash countless times over the years, how he must have been scared, in the dark, driving quickly down a dangerous mountain road, drunk, hitting the lamppost with such force it cracked his face open and left him in a coma, left him with a scarred and new face. I had whispered in his ear so many times, *I'm sorry*, from hundreds of miles away. I should have gone to visit after Martha and my mother sat me down to tell me about the accident. I didn't because we were broken up and I just believed that it was the best thing to do, because they said not to visit.

"She took me to a hotel once, before the accident. She wanted to have sex with me. I was drunk. I remember her on the bed, naked, and she tried …" He recounted the story as if he had been waiting to get it off his chest, this confession, though it wasn't his crime.

"You were a boy, Clint," I said, not sure if people had ever told him that. I didn't ask, didn't ask how he dealt with those feelings or memories. I didn't want to hold it all, only to know, to really hear it, from him. But the details were hard to listen to.

Had she been found out, she might have gone to jail. My mother had put the keys in his hands and told him to drive, to leave the apartment so no one would know he had been there. I had learned enough.

Clint used to say, "Your mother knows we kiss. She asked what we do together. I told her we kissed, that was all. Your mother's sick."

I didn't know how to pick up on the cues then. I should have recognized them, but I was too close, couldn't fathom that my own mother would have sex with my boyfriend.

I wasn't ready to hear what Martha told me, but it didn't matter to her. She needed to confess, needed forgiveness. There was no thought about how the telling would impact me. Martha was a trusted adult who had known about my mother's pedophilia and had done nothing. And while my mother was the orchestrator, the perpetrator of the crimes, Martha was a bystander. Clint was right that my mother would have been charged had it been current day, but so, too, would Martha.

I decided to leave Montreal. The city brought tragedy.

Lou was so angry, and rightfully. I was leaving her without a roommate, without rent. And I couldn't tell her what had happened, but said I had to go when the festival ended.

I rented a van and took off with a hired mover who schlepped my belongings for me. I went back to Toronto and found a bachelor apartment in the classifieds of a newspaper, a small walk-up off of Broadview, across from the park. I loved it, with its built-in Murphy bed and claw-foot tub. It was home. I would finally live alone, though it took weeks to get a phone because at the time, Bell Canada wouldn't rent a phone line to a minor. I had to argue with them endlessly about the need for a phone. Nothing was ever simple, not even getting a phone when under the age of nineteen in Ontario. I had to scrap for everything in the world, but that was okay because I was a scrapper.

I literally took to brawling on occasion; if I felt threatened or saw other girls or children being threatened, a beast came out of me I didn't even know existed. Once a man was so closely following me on the street, I felt him. After a block I dropped to the ground on all fours and loudly growled up at him like rabid dog. He retreated, looking at me like I was crazy, which I likely was. Another night I was at a lesbian bar, mixing booze with drugs. I didn't make it off the dance floor on my own, and I was just as wild when some men tried to pick me up from my nesting place on the concrete floor. It was instinctive, my response to perceived physical threats by men, which triggered everything in me, reminded me of my father. Every nerve in my body was hard-wired to expect danger. This protective internal beast often kept me safe, but it sometimes created more trouble than I could manage.

# CHAPTER TWENTY-ONE

"JOANNE, ARE YOU AWAKE? Do you know how you got here?" asked a woman staring at me from above. I was in a bed, wrists bound to bars that gave off a metallic taste and smell that made my stomach flip. The room slowly came into focus.

My voice cracked and I coughed. "I'm thirsty."

"Here." The woman brought a cup of water to my lips.

I took a sip through the straw and coughed a bit more. I was in a hospital, again, seemed to be fated to hospitals for some reason or another.

"I was called in to give an assessment," the woman said.

I tried to pull my hands free. "Why are these things on my wrists? Take them off."

"I'll get security to remove them, but I need to know you aren't going to hurt anyone or yourself."

*Is that a joke?* "But why are these on?" *If you don't take these off . . .*

"You don't remember?"

"It wasn't my fault," I said.

I had gone to a lesbian bar the night before, drinking and

dancing. I'd collapsed on the dance floor after taking too many pills mixed with alcohol. I was brought in after fighting the ambulance driver. I hadn't wanted to go to the hospital.

"My name is Alice."

She had short spiked hair and blue eyes and wore a necklace in the shape of a woman's body and swirly earrings with little green stones in the centre of each. Her voice was soothing. "Why don't you tell me what happened last night?"

"I didn't mean to hurt myself or hit that ambulance guy. I don't like being held or restrained." I paused. "I wasn't trying to kill myself. I would have found a better way — jump in front of a subway, or knife or something more ... lethal."

The mattress under my body was hard and my lungs felt constricted, sore. "I promise not to hurt you or myself. Can I get these off, please?" I knew the rules. Don't fuck with authority when your hands are bound; you'll lose.

She looked into my eyes, maybe looking for the rabid girl. I was tempted to scream but I knew it wouldn't be one of my brighter moves so I tried to control my panic. She was soft, gentle. I needed to figure out if she was a wolf, but mostly I needed the restraints to be removed.

"Please ..."

"I'll be right back." Alice left me alone and then returned with a security guard, who undid my wrists and waited with us. I didn't say anything, just grabbed my arms and hands, rubbed my wrists. The guard made me uncomfortable and I wouldn't break eye contact with him.

"You can leave now," Alice told him, as if reading my mind.

Security turned and walked out of the room.

"Are you going to commit me? I don't need that. I need to be out. My mom tried to have me committed not too long ago."

"What happened with your mother?"

I didn't want to say, just enough for her to know I wasn't "bad," wasn't the horrible child my mother tried to make me out to be. I forgot that she was a stranger who knew nothing, but I was so used to being seen as a bad girl that I thought it was visible somehow, my badness. Deflection was my mother's art, her craft; she was very good at getting people to believe I was a horrible daughter.

*Say something else.* The voice inside my head was amplified. I could hear the phrase repeat itself over and over loudly, SAY SOMEHTING ELSE.

"I … had a … an eating problem, but I wasn't living at home anymore. Why should she get to do something like that to me, have me committed?" Parental control should cease when a mother sends a child packing. I just didn't know what to tell Miss Alice.

"I'm grown enough. I'm eighteen now."

"You want to tell me more?" Alice asked, her voice soothing.

I didn't want to say more. Speaking never led to anything good, but I had a sudden urge to hold her even though I didn't know her. There was something warm about her, softness in a place with sharp angled walls, diseased and depressed people. I pretended Alice was a warm blanket, but I didn't dare reach out to touch her for comfort. Instead I answered, hoping she would see me.

"Are you okay?" Alice asked after a long silence.

"Yeah. Believe it or not, I was just trying to have a good time. I haven't been back long in Toronto and I went to a bar to have fun." And then I decided to say the words. "I'm a lesbian, ya know, and I'm okay with it." I was defensive, trying to see if she would prefer not to talk to me. "Normal" people often got weird with these types of things.

"I'm a lesbian, too."

"Oh … well … you don't look like a lesbian." I was caught off guard, didn't realize lesbians might be everywhere. I had seen gay women only in bars, not in the light of day where ordinary people had ordinary jobs. It was a first and I was a fool, a young uninformed fool with a big mouth. "Oh, sorry … I didn't mean that in a bad way or anything, just that the lesbians I've met all don't dress so … work-ish." *Idiot.* "Oh, that sounds stupid, you're a doctor.…"

"No, it's okay. You can say what you like. I'm not offended." Alice smiled.

The room was brightly lit, cramped, and uncomfortable.

"I don't want to be here." I meant it. "I just wanted to forget, to dance."

Alice calmly waited for me to say more.

"I'm on my own. I'm all I've got and I can't get locked up," I said with tears beginning to fall.

"I don't want you to stay in the hospital if you feel like you are well enough to leave on your own, if you are not going to hurt yourself."

I didn't say anything, just sat there and cried. After another long silence, I spoke. "My father beat me and my mother set it up. She wanted to watch."

"I'm so sorry."

"I couldn't help my sisters."

I was tired of carrying everything, siblings, memories, all cluttered up inside, stacked on top of each other, and I was beginning to leak, couldn't stop myself from spilling. Memories passed through me and in me like a holy ghost after being fully dunked in deep water.

"Do you want to tell me more?"

I couldn't talk about Clint, about sexual abuse, or what my mother did to me, to him. It was too much. I shook, tried to calculate the options of my situation, whether talking might convince Alice to change her mind about letting me out. I was afraid to say too much, wanted her to know I was functional, capable, even if I didn't look it. In my head the words repeated themselves: *My father was a monster.*

*My mother was obsessed with me. She had sex with Clint. It's my fault.*

"The show must go on," I whispered to myself, the mantra I had practised for years. It eased my mind, kept me in the present, focused.

"I wonder if you would be interested in seeing me privately? I have some spots available on a sliding scale," Alice said.

"What's a sliding scale?" It sounded musical, like the G could slide down to the C chord.

"Oh, it means that my fee runs up to sixty dollars an hour depending on what you can afford and there is a spot at the bottom end of the scale if you need."

"You mean, like five bucks?" I rubbed my eyes and face dry, needing a cigarette.

She looked at me and said, "Sure, if that's what you can afford to pay, then five dollars an hour will be just fine. But how about we start at no dollars an hour and see if you want to continue after a few sessions."

"Seriously. Is that for real?"

"Yes, for real. Why don't we start on Monday?" She handed me her card. "I'm going to sign the release form. You're free to go, but I would like to set up an appointment today for next week, and if you are strong enough to go home, then you can. Is there someone you want me to call?"

"No, I'll be okay," I said. "Umm ... thanks, Alice, or Mrs. ... I'm supposed to call you Alice?"

"Yes, Alice is good." She walked away and closed the door behind her.

My head hurt, as if I needed to tape skin to my brain to hold it all in again. This talk thing could get tricky.

But a doctor lesbian. Huh.

# CHAPTER
# TWENTY-TWO

"THE ROLE IS FOR a young, feisty girl ... a boxer, a ... tomboy."

"You mean a lesbian?" I asked my agent on the phone while she stumbled over the words. Suddenly, I couldn't stop saying it, and if it were possible to turn all characters into lesbians, I would have. The Bionic Woman, definite lesbian. Linda Carter had to be, as far as I was concerned. All superhero women must have been lesbians. And my childhood idol, Jodie Foster, could be nothing but, in my mind, even if she wouldn't say it.

*Lesbian*, a beautiful word even though so many tossed it around like it was something dirty. Martha once said that the word *lesbian* was an ugly word, that she didn't like it. I called her homophobic and she raged at me for suggesting she was.

I liked belonging to something so edgy sounding and fiercely female. The word rolled off my tongue as I stared at myself in the mirror and looked for the lesbian, every time I said it with a newfound confidence, a word that so many despised and I adored, *les-bi-an*. Did I look like one? Would people notice something new in me, like with a haircut or a new outfit? A rite of passage?

"Well, I don't think the girl is gay...." my agent said on the other end of the phone.

"You mean *lesbian*."

"Anyway, she's not *that*, and it's with Carla Spencer, a great filmmaker, and I think if you got this part, it would be good for your career. You'd meet some new people, get out there. It's at a new film school."

"For sure I'll be there. Thanks," I said and hung up the phone. I ran around my bachelor apartment looking for my pictures and resumé, pulled down my Murphy bed from the wall, and bounced on the mattress, did somersaults over the top of the bed, then pretended to box. Ha! Lesbian.

The moment I saw the director, I instantly fell into stupid and the nerves kicked in. I convinced myself that she was a lesbian before I knew her, and I wanted to play this role, no matter the content. Carla had blue eyes and long dirty-blond hair and wore jeans. I was wearing jeans with the image of Jimmy Dean hand-painted down one of the legs, a black leather jacket, and a T-shirt that said *Fuck you* on it.

"It takes balls walking in here with a shirt like that on," the director said. She was smiling, her eyes familiar, like someone I had known before, or maybe it was the way she looked at me, as if she knew me. I was bold in my clothing choice but could find nothing to say with my numb tongue, a rush of heat moving up into my face.

"Well, how about we start."

"Yeah ... oh yeah ... I'm ready," I said after taking my place on my mark before the camera.

"Oh, before we roll, can you box?"

"Sure ... well, if you want me to, that is," I smiled at her, then lifted my hands in the air and started to jump back and forth, jabbing my fists into the air like I had at home.

She smiled back at me in a way that was too intimate for what we were doing. I couldn't help but stare at her a second too long.

"Camera's rolling, so ... anytime," she said, clicking a pen with her thumb, waiting for me to begin.

# CHAPTER TWENTY-THREE

"I THINK I'M FALLING in love."

I sat on the floor in Alice's office with cushions all around me. It was a small office with a desk, carpeted floor, two chairs, very little on the walls. I preferred to sit on the ground. I couldn't fall far.

Alice was the opposite of my mother. Never scrutinized my look or my body size, never expected anything of me. I tried to get her to dislike me or push me away, but she never did. Just kept that therapy gaze, eye contact that was impressive, never veered, freakish almost, like a plastic doll with eyes that never blinked.

Alice smiled. "Tell me about her." Her green earrings swinging beneath her lobes every time she moved or spoke was hypnotic.

"Well, she's a lot older than me. Actually, she's my director for this film I'm doing." I picked at the fraying material of my jeans over my knee, pulling the faded threads and making a larger hole while I spoke, my face turning red.

"How much older?"

"I don't know ... maybe fifteen years," I said.

I looked up to see Alice's expression. Her smile disappeared briefly, though she almost immediately recovered her therapy face. But I did catch her initial reaction, that moment of disapproval.

"Does she have feelings for you, too?"

"I'm pretty sure. We spend a lot of time hanging out together after rehearsal and talking about our lives. We've been to this pub a couple of times and ... I think she likes me, yeah."

She did, I knew. I couldn't tell Alice that Carla would tenderly touch my hands or face and look at me longingly, dreamlike, misty. But I knew.

"Do you think it's okay for thirty-three-year-old men to date eighteen- or nineteen-year-old women? I know you like her, but do you think it's a fair or an equal beginning?" Alice asked, her therapy face firmly intact.

"She doesn't feel older."

"Have you ever dated an older person before?" Alice asked.

The good thoughts were interrupted by a question I cared not to answer, or could not.

"I'm going to ask you to think about this. Why do you think a thirty-three-year-old woman feels confident about dating an eighteen-year-old?"

*Don't.* Something stirred inside my body, another part of me that wanted me to be quiet. I wanted to tell her about my mother, but I couldn't, as if that other part had a rope inside my belly pulling the door to my vocal chords shut so I couldn't speak. But I did not want Carla to be compared to my mother. She was nothing like her. Carla wasn't my mother, so I believed it was equitable because I was old enough and believed I was smart enough.

I just didn't know I wasn't mature enough. There was a difference. I wanted love. I had wished for it my whole life and believed it had arrived. I was too young for Carla. Perhaps Carla knew it, but it wouldn't stop what was about to occur between us. I had agency as a young adult, and there was no stopping the train.

# What

## PART THREE

# I Knew

# CHAPTER
# TWENTY-FOUR

## 2002 — Princess Margaret Hospital

BEFORE I GO to the hospital for another talk, I need answers. We had moved Mother into an east-end apartment in Toronto soon after she arrived from BC, a beautiful place with large windows overlooking a ravine with trees, greenery, and birds.

I go there now to find journals, notes, anything I can. Maybe I'll find her birth certificate or old letters from when she was a teenager, pictures, things each of us tucks away in secret.

My mother's history is a mystery. She never spoke of her family, only said that they were very poor and that her mother frequently beat and punished her. Mother had to go to school with the nuns, who were apparently just as cruel. That's all I was ever really told.

I open the glass doors of the bookcases that hold hundreds of books on wooden shelves, including an old leather-bound Bible with a satin string for keeping track of the page. I open my mother's Bible to the marked page and look at a couple of the headings in bold black print: THE TRUTH SHALL MAKE YOU FREE

and ABRAHAM'S SEED AND SATAN. There are other books —
books about Princess Diana, books by Stephen King, cookbooks,
and even her own recipe book for the restaurant she had in BC.
Inside her recipe book are a few placemats with her restaurant logo
on them: "Homestead, home cooking."

I hold books by their spines and covers and dangle them upside
down in an attempt to find hidden papers or pictures, as if magical
memories might fall out and I'll be able to see them. I go through
rows and rows of books this way and disappointedly find nothing.
When I open the closet in her office, I find dozens of laminated posters and pictures from my old shows going back to my childhood.

Mother's computer sits on her desk. I push the power button
and wait for the green light. I notice a little red-and-gold-striped
case with a handle and flip it open. Inside sit all the 45s from my
childhood, from dance lessons, stuff my mother purchased about
how to tap. I pull the 45s out — ABBA, Barbra Streisand, the
Beatles, and, of course, Barry Manilow, favourites that I listened to
on my plastic record player to under the porch when I was a child.

I turn to the computer, the monitor bright with symbols and files.

Perfect. I sit down in the soft chair and begin to search, clicking
on icons until I find her work files. Boring. Then I open her email
program and browse the trash folder, which hasn't been erased from
the hard drive. I start to read the emails in sequence and realize that
I am reading messages from different men she met on a dating site.

Then I open one she sent to a man that says, "Here is a picture
of me taken only a few years ago. I know I am a bit younger in it,
but it's one of my best shots and I thought you might like it." The
message is signed "Lisa." I scroll down to look at the picture, and
there it is taking up the whole screen, a picture taken of me when I
was thirteen, a headshot from my first photo session with Martha.
I stand up and pace while I stare at the image. I can't fucking
believe this. How could she?

I sit back down and keep clicking and reading. I come to another image of me, a different shot from the same photo session, but this time her name is Janet and she claims she is twenty-three years old.

I stand up and walk back to the closet to look through boxes and letters. I find divorce papers and newspaper clippings, old black-and-white photos. I open a large wooden drawer that holds dozens of envelopes and photograph albums and pull them all out. Everything is strewn on the carpet. I dump out an envelope and there are black-and-white baby pictures of Lou, Sadie, Diego, and me. Then I dump another envelope and stop.

I put my hand over my mouth. There are grainy coloured photographs of my mother and one of Clint back in our old apartment, and another laminated photo of him on a wooden board. I throw it on the floor. The phone rings. I jump up, startled. It rings and rings and I run out of the room looking for something in her kitchen to drink, anything, a beer, liquor, anything, but there is nothing. I walk back into the office and look at the computer screen with the picture of me, sent to her twenty-something-year-old boyfriend and the other men. Fuck. She is still doing this, still, in her sixties. How could she use my image in this way, a picture of her thirteen-year-old daughter to attract men?

It's time. I need to know a few things. I leave the apartment as fast as I can and make my way to the hospital.

It is quiet on the ward. There aren't many visitors when the sun is up. I go to her room, determined to challenge her, to make her tell me the truth. I reach her door and halt. She doesn't see me. She's sitting up in her bed with her food tray in front of her, her fingers delicately playing the keys of an invisible piano while her head sways back and forth to a tune only she can hear.

I walk in and her fingers fall away from her tray. Her face widens into a smile, and I know she is losing her grip. I lunge right in about Martha and Clint. I don't want to lose my resolve. "You need to tell me what happened when I was a teenager."

"What?"

"What did you and Martha talk about? What happened that night?"

She looks at me as if she does not know the night in question. Perhaps she doesn't.

"The night of the accident."

The smile on my mother's face quickly vanishes. "I told Martha everything and she betrayed me. She poisoned your head," Mother says, straightening her back with a small burst of energy.

The nurses walk by and stare into the room. I wait for them to pass before I answer. "She did not. God, what are you talking about?" I stand near her bed, intent on getting answers.

"Nothing … just forget it. Did you come all the way here to jump on me?"

"No, don't do that!" I want her to stop. She always changes the subject or looks away.

"She knew! She knew, okay?" Mother picks up her plastic cup to take a sip of water, stalling.

"And?"

"And, and, AND. You think she was so perfect. Martha, Martha, Martha!" Mother says loudly, suddenly repeating everything in threes.

"I know what happened the night Clint went to your apartment."

"No, you do not!" She points her finger at me, then puts her cup down.

But I was at her apartment. The blood hadn't even been properly washed from the wall that night. It was Clint's blood. She and Martha both lied, and she is still lying now.

Mom coughs in her bed, pulls her water cup back to her lips. I wait, then continue. "Martha told me things about what happened. So did Steffin and —"

"But you were sick, throwing up and not eating, or killing yourself —"

"Stop it! Stop doing that. Stop trivializing my life." Her carefully chosen words are meant to diminish, phrases she throws around: *starving, killing yourself.* Deflection. I choke back rage and the urge to scream at the top of my lungs. I stare at my shoes, the floor, anywhere but at her. It hasn't taken much for her to make me feel like a five-year-old again and I don't want her to see the child in me.

"Stop doing what?" she asks back, as if she doesn't know.

"Belittling me. This isn't about my eating. Why can't you just answer the fucking question?"

"Don't talk to me like that. Yes, Martha, then. Martha wasn't what you think," Mother says.

I don't think much of Martha. "I need you to tell me the truth. I need to know what happened with Clint." *There is no time left, Mother. You are dying. Speak.* "What did you do to him?"

She looks at me like she's thinking *How dare you ask such a thing?* Indignant, her eyes lock onto mine. The room seems to get smaller, windows covered, ceiling low, little space between my mother's bed and me.

"What happened between you and Clint, Mom?" I meet her gaze and hold it without flinching.

"I loved him," she says with a pointed finger, as if there is something wrong with me for even asking, as she once again tries to shut the conversation down. That finger threat with those eyes often got me to clam up when I was young, the *just you wait 'til your father gets home* look.

"Is that what you call it?" My voice shakes ever so slightly.

"I loved him."

"He was a teenager. He was my boyfriend, a kid."

"I never touched him, or you."

"Don't lie."

"Is that what this is about?" she asks, surprised, changing the subject. "Is this why you haven't seen me in all these years?"

Is she kidding? Yes, partly. Isn't it a good enough reason? I think molesting your child's adolescent boyfriend qualifies. If only it were just that.

"Is that the only reason you left me?" My mom asks again when I don't respond, as if she has been the victim of neglect.

"How do you do that? Seem innocent, trying to make me feel bad, always turning things around? You were the mother, not me. You sent me to Toronto, remember? I didn't leave you. And no, it's not the only reason I stopped talking to you, if that's your question, but I guess you've conveniently forgotten everything, or maybe you really just forget. I know what happened." I stop and face her. Her vulnerability is not my concern now.

She stayed and I wasn't there anymore. She could do what she wanted. Free rein, no more pesky daughter to slip the noose around her neck or kick her out of her room, pushing her to be a better mother. She packed me up and made it all look so great from the outside, sending her kid to another city to go to an arts school, while she was manipulating and seducing Clint at home in Montreal.

I inch closer to her bed. "Steffin knew, didn't he? He told me he saw you at the apartment and that you nearly pushed him out of a window."

Steffin told me one day while he was on a visit to Toronto during Pride. He said he had been alone with my mother one evening. Her hatred for him had escalated to new heights, and she put her fingers around his throat and threatened to push him out the window where they stood. She blamed him for taunting Clint, blamed him because he knew about her, and she wanted him silenced.

"He's a liar! He was the one that caused it. He was the one spreading rumours."

"You choked him."

Steffin tried to tell. Steffin could read people, push people. "He told me you choked him and nearly pushed him. That wasn't a lie." I am now standing over her, my hands clenched around the bars that hold her in.

"I should have pushed him."

"Mom!" It slips out again, the word *mom*, but I don't care. I am in shock that that sentiment, those words, could easily fall from her lips, that she hated a teen that much.

"I'm sorry," she says and grabs my hand like a Venus flytrap.

*For what?* I pull away. Her hand falls to her side.

"I'll be back. I need to go get a drink. I'll see you later," I say and slowly make my way to the visiting room and sit by a window, looking out over the bare trees in the courtyard. Surely there had been a time when she was young that she dreamed of more? At what point did her conscience start to slip through her fingers?

I don't know what to do with myself, wonder if there were other young people my mother tried to seduce, maybe other friends of mine or even Lou's or Diego's.

A woman enters the lounge, drying her tears with her sleeve.

"Do you want me to leave the lounge?" I ask.

"No, it's fine, I'm sorry. Didn't mean to bother you."

"You're not ... I was just resting, thinking."

"I've seen you here before." She sits across from me.

"Yeah, my mother has been here for a while. Uterine cancer."

"I'm sorry. My husband is here. Eye cancer."

"Sorry."

"I just don't know what I'd do without him, ya know?" She is soft-spoken.

"I understand. I'm sorry."

"Oh, of course you do. It must be hard for you to face losing your mother."

I look at her and accept her idea of what losing my mother would be like. I have heard these types of phrases my entire life. People assumed a relationship existed, or that we were connected in ways other mothers and daughters were, during holidays, Mother's Day, or every day. I rarely corrected anyone. It was easier. The idea of *mother* was sacred to many, or at least the illusion of it. Pedophilia was not the first thing that came to mind for most when thinking about mothers.

# CHAPTER
# TWENTY-FIVE

1986

OPENING NIGHT OF Carla's film was held at a beautiful mansion with large, luscious gardens and fountains — a fairy-tale castle fit for kings and queens. I was the lesbian Cinderella in pants and leathers trying to fit in with a crowd of invited artists and intellectuals, the men in black tie, the women in heels and dresses, with their faces perfectly painted masks.

That perfect femininity and controlled beauty always intimidated me. I didn't understand why, but I knew that they were the desired construct of *woman*, which meant I was undesirable. I wasn't sure what Carla saw in me. My stomach ached and I felt out of place in the circle of filmmakers.

"I can't watch the show with everyone. I'm going to the projection booth," Carla said in the bathroom, visibly nervous as she paced in front of me. Her hair had been gelled so that it stuck up on the top of her head in a horrible mullet. She was wearing more makeup than I had ever seen her wear, and she was as nervous as I was. Spontaneously, I grabbed her hand and we stood close to each other, face to face, almost hugging, her fingers in mine. Her breath was hot on my skin.

"It's okay … don't worry, they're going to love it because you wrote it and because you're brilliant," I said, still holding her hand. She didn't let go.

"You think? You're so sweet." Carla dropped her head on my shoulder. She was wearing a black miniskirt and jacket and smelled like pineapple, alcohol, and perfume. Her hair touched my neck and a surge of electricity passed through me. I pulled her in closer for a hug.

"Well, we better get out of here before someone thinks something is going on." Carla pulled herself away slowly, then opened the door. "Come find me when the screening is over, okay?" She disappeared.

I did a little dance and stared at myself in the large bathroom mirror before running out to take my seat.

Carla and I were the only two left in the building after drinking and partying all night at the bash. I requested the Pretenders' "I'll Stand by You," and played air guitar for Carla, singing along to the whole song. I belted out the lyrics, half kneeling on the ground in front of her, in love, not caring who was left at the party, my energy and Carla's like a cosmic collision, a comet crashing into Earth full speed ahead.

I sipped my beer and looked at her on the couch where she sat looking back at me. I got up to sit beside her and let my hand fall near her thigh.

"I have the key to this place, you know. It's four in the morning," she said.

"What do you want to do?" I asked, my hand touching her thigh on the couch, hidden where no one could see, just in case.

"I'm heading out," said the director of program. "You can stay, but make sure to lock the door, Carla," he said as if he knew we weren't going to leave.

"Yup, we'll be going soon. Just going to have one more beer and a few more songs."

"Good work tonight, Joanne, Carla. G'night." He left.

"Is it really just us left in this mansion?" I asked.

"Yeah ... want to grab another drink and go upstairs on the veranda?" Carla put her fingers through my hair for the first time. "You're so fucking cute. I couldn't fucking stand watching you sing along with Chrissie Hynde and not kiss you."

I looked at her, my heart in my throat.

"Have you ever been with a woman before?" Carla asked after we had climbed the circular staircase to the top floor of the building. We walked down the hall, hands clasped together, and found a large darkened room with large bay windows and double doors that led to a veranda, a beautiful porch with the moon above and the fountain below, a constant flow, the sound of water like a song playing just for us as the trees whistled in tune in the green evening with the smell of summer all around.

"It's so romantic here, don't you think?" she asked.

"Yeah, it's beautiful ... and no, I have never been with a woman before." I didn't know what to do or how. Wasn't sure if I was supposed to lead or she was. I didn't know if there were unspoken rules. I was shy, uncertain.

"Can I kiss you?" she asked, tucking strands of my long hair behind my ear, looking into my eyes while her other hand held mine.

I leaned in to kiss her without answering. We kissed tenderly and held each other's faces, hands brushing up and down backs as we kissed some more and explored with our lips, gentle, light.

"How was that?" Carla asked.

"Amazing. Can I kiss you again?" I asked, leaning in to kiss her a second time. My heart trembled, wanting to feel hers close to mine, against my chest.

After we left the veranda, we made a mattress out of couch cushions and held one another, kissing softly until we fell asleep, arms entangled, bodies curled together, a perfect fit. When we woke, we stared into each other's eyes, glossy, giddy, brushing each other's palms with our fingertips.

"I always wanted to kiss you, but thought maybe I was the only one that had feelings," I said.

"I had a crush on you the minute I saw you in that audition, with that leather jacket and your Jimmy Dean jeans and those big eyes," she said back.

"I think I did, too, that first day. I was convinced about you. I was so nervous and I just wanted you to pick me, to cast me, kiss me."

"You're a kid."

"Ha. My first boyfriend said that, too."

"Ha ha ha, shut it." Carla kissed me again.

A breeze came through the window, sending a chill into the room. I pulled Carla in closer, until we faced each other. I didn't know that loving a woman would align my insides like a photograph coming into focus. "Can I look at you, just your eyes and your face? I just want to see you," I said gently cupping her face, tracing the lines on her skin, the tiny scar near her right brow, the shape of her eyes. I was afraid she looked a little sad, but thought it was just my own insecurities, my own self-doubt. I wanted everything bad to recede. I kissed her forehead and we held each other close, as if we were one solid, strong body filled with tenderness.

"Do you seduce all your actresses?" I asked, sipping cognac in the pub a few days later, "I want to know everything."

Carla lifted one side of her mouth in a half smile. "No, only you. I've never been with any of my actresses before."

"Oh bull."

"No, really…"

"What about jailbait?"

"Again, only you." She sipped her drink. All I saw were her lips, the small crease along her neck, her collarbone half covered by a white cotton shirt under a worn leather jacket with a painted eagle on the back. I touched her legs under the table with my hand, over her knee. The old Irish pub was dark, with middle-aged drunken patrons hanging from barstools with pints. There were no women here, let alone lesbians, except for Carla and me. We rattled through all our favourites: De Niro, Judi Dench, chocolate ice cream, Frida Kahlo, Bette Davis, sleeping on the left or the right, Joan Jett, Audre Lorde, Sylvia Plath.

"How can you call yourself an actress without having seen *Days of Wine and Roses*?" she asked.

We were drunk on whisky and repressed kisses.

"Pat Parker," I said.

"Don't know him."

"It's a *her*. And how can you not know Pat Parker?" I teased. "Famous poet? Activist? Black Panther?" She shook her head no. "There is more to life then movies, you know." I wanted to touch her and hold her in public, but I knew better.

"No, there isn't," Carla said.

"You're missing out on real revolutionaries … they're not just in moviesss." I slurred a little. "What about how we live? Why it's so fucked up that gay people live like we do, in hiding?"

"The world doesn't like hookers or fags —"

"We're not that," I said, not because I had anything against hookers or fags, but it felt like a slur and I wanted no part of that. "We're just people."

"You're naive. But sweet. Come on, let's get out of here and grab a little food," Carla said.

We stumbled out of the bar and fell off the curb together without noticing, missed the whole step down entirely and dropped onto the road with a thud. We couldn't get up, we were laughing so hard. Carla's pants ripped at the knees. I kissed the flesh exposed on her leg, then moved up to her lips, there in front of a tree planted in a patch of soil surrounded by concrete. She pulled me up and away from the street. We grabbed a slice from the three-for-one pizza place below my studio on Parliament Street. We walked up the steps to my room, where we left the uneaten slice of pie on the table, kicked off our shoes and clothes, and collapsed into bed in hunger for each other.

Carla and I started spending all our free time together. On the days I knew I would see her she would say, "Don't eat today because I want to take you to dinner and I want you to eat with me, not push the food around the plate."

I would only have dinner with her if I had not eaten lunch, and sometimes I didn't want to have sex with her if I'd eaten. I felt too heavy with food. Not eating allowed me to float, disassociate. Sex was intimate, messy, with uncontrolled feelings I did not want to expose, not even with Carla. I couldn't fully let go, and the nagging voice inside my head was like a tripwire, sometimes sounding like my mother, words incessantly rotating in my head, like *fat* or *Don't cry* or *Do you love me*? I didn't want her in my head. It was exhausting. Keeping an internal world secret and suppressing childhood memories took a lot of energy. I could only share stories of my childhood with Carla in short bursts, unable to tell all. But I would, eventually.

Carla was just trying to enjoy herself with me like normal grown-ups did, except I wasn't *normal* and I wasn't entirely grown-up. I was a baby dyke. That's what her roommate called me when I went knocking.

"Carla, the baby dyke's here," the singer with a famous song said from behind the door. She was beautiful, mature, and confident. I wanted to tell her how much I loved her music, but I stayed silent, embarrassed by my youth somehow and wishing I could appear more adult. After all, I was simply a baby dyke to her, not so much a grown-up lesbian.

Navigating the world of lesbians could be tricky. There were all these power dynamics to adjust to, like in any family or tribe. Especially at the lesbian bar in Toronto we referred to as the Hose, where everyone seemed to know each other, a large dysfunctional family that included the cocaine-addicted DJ who looked like a female version of Steven Tyler from Aerosmith, the bartenders who could have picked me up by their pinky fingers, large and strong looking, and the patrons, from the butch bull dykes to the pixie queers to the softest and tenderest femmes. Some were young like me, sometimes carded or snuck in by others. It was the only place for women to be where they could feel safe, to dance, to hide. Sexual energy filled the bar, especially when a slow song was playing and women crammed in together on the floor, swaying and kissing. In the bathrooms, we all knew if the door wouldn't open that people were either having sex or doing drugs, or both. Someone would inevitably get angry and knock. "Open the damn door and take it home. People have to use the toilet."

Women cruised all the time. I felt the eyes of women, usually older, following me like I was fresh meat. And when those eyes locked on me, it was like they were undressing me. I was ridiculously uncomfortable, uncertain of my place in the world of lesbians, not knowing if I was supposed to be a femme or a butch or if those roles mattered anymore. It wasn't the 1950s, but lesbians came in all sorts of packages, and I just didn't know what sort was mine. But I knew that the women were strong, even the softest ones who sat in corners nursing drinks. And the ones who bound their breasts and wore suits and ties, who stood tall and dignified even though they could be jumped at night or harassed on the outside of the women's bar, out in the jungle of our city where queers were still vilified. And especially the butches, the ones who did not pass or try to. They were the bravest of us, out there for all to see.

# CHAPTER TWENTY-SIX

I WAS PRACTISING for a part I was hired to play on *Street Legal*, a fifteen-year-old blind prostitute. I borrowed a cane from the Canadian National Institute for the Blind and wore dark-tinted glasses, then spent the week on the streets with my props, pretending to walk without sight in the downtown core, at crosswalks, on sidewalks, and in public spaces.

Carla had a little Havanese, a small teddy bear–type dog with black and white fur that she brought everywhere she could with her. One night we had the dog with us and we really wanted to go into a pub but knew we couldn't take him in, so I put my glasses on, held my cane, and grabbed the leash.

"Can we come in? Can I bring my guide dog?" I asked, thinking we would get turned away because no one used a Havanese as a guide dog, but the wait staff let us in. We spent most of our time giggling because I had to pretend I was blind all night, which became harder to do the more beer I drank. For a girl who had never made it through high school, I was certain that intelligence did not equal academic achievements, and if college kids working at bars thought Havanese were trained dogs for the visually impaired, then I was going to do well in the world.

The following day I practised with my cane on Bay Street. A group of four teenage boys passed me, calling me four eyes and every other name they could think of. I whipped off my shades and started to chase them up the street toward Bloor, trying to hit them with my cane. "Who you calling four eyes, you fuckers?" I raged, swinging the cane as they ran from me screaming.

"Holy shit, she's crazy!"

Carla and I laughed ourselves to sleep after I retold the story a second and third time, each time with a new detail about how their arms were up in the air or the high-pitched screams they made. I loved that laughter was the last thing we heard from each other before sleep, stroking hair, bodies entwined, giggling into quiet before dreamland. We were still enjoying the bubble we had created, living inside our own little black-and-white movie together, in hiding. I would keep our new relationship under wraps, which at first wasn't hard to do. We were used to compartmentalizing, and I was used to embodying other characters as an actor, abandoning myself for make-believe. But abandoning my own truth to keep someone else's secret would prove to be devastating.

# CHAPTER
# TWENTY-SEVEN

I WAS GROWING UP and there were expectations of me as a female actor. The world of make-believe was beginning to cause unrest, internal conflict with my identity as an androgynous woman. Al Waxman cast me as Maggie in *Maggie's Secret*, a CBS Schoolbreak Special, the story of a girl with two alcoholic parents and a sexually abusive father. After reading the script, I knew I was meant to be Maggie, could express all those pent-up feelings from childhood and get paid for it. Good medicine.

*Maggie's Secret* was initially written by Margot Kidder, a fact that slipped from the page; the production ended up with male names on all the titles. I wanted to know the truth behind the story, but I didn't dare ask. I knew only that Al Waxman was directing and I was hired. I wanted to speak with Margot because I felt like she understood. She was Lois Lane, an idol, a truth-teller. But I was told not to mention her name. I spoke to her in my head because I hadn't met another female actor who wrote these types of stories. Instead, I was surrounded by men who wanted me to tell the story their way.

I had a type of bravery, or stubbornness you could call it. After a wardrobe meeting I was ushered into Al's office. He closed the door and screamed at me.

"They wanted to fire you, Joanne, because you won't wear the miniskirt," he said angrily, sitting behind his desk. "I had to stick up for you and tell them that I knew you were the right one for the part, that you would wear the clothes. If you don't want to get fired, Joanne, you have to compromise or you will lose the part."

Al was like a father and larger than life, a talented man whom many adored. He was Lieutenant Bert Samuels of *Cagney & Lacey*, but he was particularly kind to me, the closest I might get to having a film father like all my movie mothers. But I pushed back, like any child.

"But … why can't I do that scene without having to wear such a small skirt?"

"It's the network, Joanne. I don't care, but you have to do this. I won't be able to fight for you if you keep saying no."

I loved him even though I didn't like what he was saying and he had no idea how much I truly hated being feminine, being forced to wear clothes that made me feel like an imposter, even if it was for a character. I couldn't fight the man who stuck up for me, and I didn't want to lose my role. I wanted to be Maggie.

Al knew somehow that I was a lesbian, maybe because his own daughter would eventually come out — and not only did she come out, but she transitioned into a man. I didn't know her at the time, but I would meet her, and I would then understand why he had fought for me.

"But, Al, why don't you wear a skirt?" I asked.

"I won't answer that" was all he said, with authority. The only way I knew how to express how I felt was to compare what it might be like for a straight male to always be asked to wear skirts or sexually revealing clothes when they were only comfortable in pants because those expressed their gender. But it wasn't expected that they should have to wear skimpy clothes.

I had to make a decision. Hollywood had no patience for feminism or young women with opinions or non-binary people. There was no language for it yet, and I could be replaced.

"Okay, Al, I'll do it," I said.

"Good girl. Now go back to wardrobe right away. They are waiting for you."

I continued to meet the demands of the industry — auditioned, worked, hid my lesbianism — but I also had enormous amounts of fun, days when I spilled my guts with laughter.

I got a part on *Men*, a show with Ted Wass and Saul Rubinek. I was beyond excited to work with Ted, whom I remembered as Danny from the comedy *Soap*. It was hard not to laugh on set working with a group of comedians, always "on." I played the precocious teen runaway on the streets of Boston. In one scene I was in bed with a man. I had little flesh-coloured strips of sticky tape over my nipples, as I was supposed to be topless and in bed with this adult. But somehow it didn't bother me, being nearly naked. No one cared on this set and none of these men tried to make a pass at me. Aside from continuing to pretend to be heterosexual, I was having the time of my life on sets.

Carla tried to cast me in another film with her while I was shooting *Men*, but they would not allow me to shoot two shows at the same time. It was another short film, one that would eventually be turned into a feature, and she would catapult herself into the film and television market, becoming a star in her own right. Her light would shine while she was in the closet, living a secretive life, and I was her secret. I was living a double life, too, but I was willing to risk it all to profess my love. I was "arriving," or so I thought. But it wasn't that simple. I was just in love for the first time with a woman. I had had two first loves, and I was hoping my second first-love relationship wouldn't end as tragically as the first, but the closet was getting too small for comfort.

# CHAPTER
# TWENTY-EIGHT

WEEKS TURNED INTO MONTHS, which turned into two years of dating. I was twenty-one years old. Carla had moved twice since we started dating and I was still in the studio on Parliament. I added new furnishings and a small pool table and filled the walls with charcoal drawings I sketched of friends from photographs or of people I'd worked with on film sets, trying to capture moments to remember. There were no phones with cameras, and film was expensive to develop, only to be used on special occasions, birthdays, wrap parties, trips.

I worked with actors and stars like Anne Meara, Amanda Plummer, Ally Sheedy, Helen Shaver, Brooke Shields, Whoopi Goldberg, Wendy Crewson, Cynthia Dale, and Marlo Thomas. Marlo was playing a role based on the life of Sharon Simone, who had survived sexual abuse by her father, a child-abuse investigator in the FBI. Being the "expert," he *expertly* knew how to get away with raping his four daughters. Meeting the real Sharon that day on set, I wanted to thank her for being so brave, but I was tongue-tied and merely shook her hand.

I was socially awkward, knew dialogue, memorized phrases that did not require sharing real stories or conversation, and wasn't good with small talk. But I truly wanted to scream at the world to wake up and get its shit together.

"I hate you," I screamed over and over at the top of my lungs at Marlo Thomas for hours on set one night, until all the desire for screaming was zapped right out of me.

"You're a star," Marlo said. "You've got something special."

I called it special "rage," but I didn't feel like a good actor, more like an imposter. I thought I was faking it, that any day someone was going to realize I was a fake, that I couldn't truly be any good at being an actor, that I only *pretended* to be good at my job. Would that make me doubly talented for impersonating an actor while auditioning and playing a role, or did it just mean I had some sort of mental illness? I settled on mental illness.

Shirley Douglas was another Canadian icon. She personified female power, but I was too young to know how she managed to achieve hers, and it was only some time later that I learned her father was one of the great Canadians who created and fought for health care in Canada, Tommy Douglas. Good genes.

All these women kept me motivated, though they didn't know it. We shared secrets about being female, about earnings, sexism, objectification.

Actors found intimacies in six-week turnovers. Nothing ever lasted in film. Relationships formed quickly and ended just as abruptly, but I was used to that as a life pattern. The women did not disappoint, no matter the false narrative of the catty woman. Hateful women existed, but I would make them invisible and focus on the loving and intelligent women — and there were plenty of those. It was the men I needed to be careful of, middle-aged actors and directors who sought us out, particularly on location, in the north of BC, or in hotel rooms in Chicoutimi, Quebec, or

Winnipeg, in those small towns where nothing remotely glamorous existed and there was too much liquor and men who were up to no good, men on location with young girls and women.

One night in Quebec, I was playing poker with two actors in their midthirties. The men had invited me to their room to play poker, which, after cocaine and too much whisky, turned into them suggesting strip poker on the carpeted floor beside the bed. I was uncomfortable but went along with it anyway, knowing that I would not reveal my flesh. By the time I had taken off my socks, jacket, and belt, had pulled my bra through the sleeves of my T-shirt, I knew it was time to go. The men were stealing glances at each other, as if I couldn't pick up on their cues. I was young, but not as naive as they thought. I bolted, felt around inside my pockets for my hotel-room key, and shut the door behind me, alone.

There was also the middle-aged, married actor who played my high-school teacher in one production, who stuck his tongue down my throat after months of friendship. Maybe I *was* naive. There were many men like this, actors, directors, producers. I was taken to a strip club in northern BC. I was a misplaced girl in a bar, watching a grown woman twirl on a pole, exposing every part of her body while I sat between our director and the lead actor, the "teacher."

"Takes a long time to be as good as she is — lotta skill," the director said in his cockney accent, turning to me. His white hair and white skin were blotchy from the days of exposure to the cold northern winter, where temperatures reached minus forty. We were all freezing.

I slept with a bottle of booze every night, and on rare occasions, I could reach Carla, thousands of kilometres away. I missed her. The night I was taken to the strip club, I fell asleep wondering how long it took to learn to point your naked leg and stretch it from a pole into the splits. I had tried to focus on her face and not her body. It was void of expression. How many years had it taken to learn that skill?

"Carla, I need to talk," I said from my hotel room in Fort Nelson. I was on my bed, the phone receiver in one hand, my other hand wrapped around a bottle. I could hear my castmates in the pool, drunk beyond my doors.

"You know it's the middle of the night, right?" she said, not mad, but I had woken her up.

"I'm sorry, Carla. I'll hang up."

"No, don't, it's okay. You okay? You drunk?"

"Yes, but it feels good to hear your voice." It was true. Her voice was soft and familiar. "I love you, Carla."

"I love you."

Even if our relationship was secret, it was still safe, warm.

"Did you shoot today?" Carla asked.

"Yeah. Depressing here. Saw a woman strip tonight and thought of you."

"What?"

"I mean … you know what I mean," I said. Many women stripped to get through college, including Carla. I changed the subject. "My mother nearly let me take my clothes off on-camera when I was a child."

"Your mother was crazy, and anyway, the only woman you need to take your clothes off for is me," Carla said.

I knew it was a joke, but it triggered something inside I could not run from. Carla was old enough to be my mother, but it wasn't that, it was the power imbalance between us, the secret. Childhood abuse was secretive, as was my relationship to Carla. I felt sick.

"I have to go." I hung up and threw up. Memories were tricky things.

When I got back from BC, Carla and I spent as much time together as we could afford, but we were rarely sober, except during the daylight hours. Carla read lines and I prepared for auditions as we snuggled under blankets watching De Niro, Foster, and Streep, alone in our cocoon.

"You talkin' to me? You talkin' to me? Well, who else you lookin' at? Huh?" I was up on my feet in my underwear and T-shirt, pointing a finger-gun as if in the scene. Carla pulled me down toward her.

"You fucking nut bar, you're never going to get a part as a Vietnam vet."

"Well, rather be the vet than be the prostitute … again. I'm sick of prostitute parts."

Where were the Mary Tyler Moore shows? Even the oldie seventies shows from my childhood had better roles: *Maude, Laverne & Shirley, One Day at a Time.*

"Well, stop acting like a thug and maybe you'll get to audition for other parts."

"Oh yeah, like Anne of Green Gables? They're not gonna hire me!" I struck a pose, then wiggled around the room before I dropped on the bed laughing. "I suppose there are other roles, like girls in the 1800s in mountain villages with a church. We should write a comedy and plant a bar like the Hose right inside the 1800s, and all the church girls come out at night to meet the butches of the 1980s."

Carla laughed, her lips lifted in one corner. I loved her lopsided smile.

"Why can't we be together more?" I asked. Normally she ignored this question, though it hovered above us like a heavy storm cloud. She looked at me lovingly, her fingers combing through my hair. I knew what it meant: it was to quiet the conversation, shift the action.

We stayed in bed on Sundays, drank coffee, read poetry to each other. I took out my copy of poems by Dylan Thomas and

Sylvia Plath. Carla read out loud, sprawled on the bed. We talked about the meaning of each sentence.

"Oh, wait." I retrieved a notepad from the top drawer of the nightstand. "I wrote this for you after you fell asleep. Tell me if you like it. 'I'll drink your tears to share the pain until your eyes are dry again. I'll never let you fall asleep without saying goodnight, without holding you tight.'"

Love felt dangerous, because now there was something to lose.

"Do you think it's possible to love someone too much?" Carla sipped water out of the jug that sat on the nightstand beside me, next to the empty Häagen-Dazs container. The window was half shut, the sun's rays shining above our faces.

"Like I love you?" I asked.

"You're such a cornball.... Do you? Do you think you love me too much?"

"No, I love you enough," I said.

"Enough for what?"

"Enough that I'd do anything for you, stay quiet for you, sing for you, even stop eating for you."

"Well, you don't have to do that for me, you dingbat, you already starve yourself." She swatted the top of my head. "I should publish the fucking book on dating someone with an eating disorder," she said as she touched my stomach, her fingers rubbing my skin.

"Ha, that's funny, and I don't have an eating disorder. I eat. Okay, I know I'm not like a regular person, but you love me, right?" I rolled on top of her, looked into her shimmering eyes. The rays of light shone on her face as the light slowly faded from the sky, from us, into dusk.

"Of course I do," Carla said, and kissed me lightly. "I just can't always be open about it, out there. I wouldn't get work if producers and companies knew I was a lesbian."

"I hate that we have to hide inside our apartments or get drunk in pubs and places where no one will know us. Makes me feel like something is wrong."

"Nothing's wrong. But people would wonder why I'm dating such a young actress, too, you know."

I slid off Carla's body, reached out toward the night table to grab a cigarette and lit up, my hands shaking until the match went out. I inhaled deeply and filled my lungs with smoke. There was the element of control between us that I didn't know how to name, her control. If I challenged it too much, it could end our relationship. Tears fell from my face as I flicked the ashes in the ashtray, looking away from her.

"Oh, come on … come here, Jimmy Dean." The nickname usually made me grin, but not then.

"I'm not a kid, Carla, and I'm not just some actress, and I don't feel bad about being a lesbian."

She blinked and looked away, folded her arms on top of herself, away from me. "Well, I can't take a chance on losing everything I've built as a director, losing everything I've worked for. Do you want me to fail?" She asked it accusingly, her body rigid. All the softness had vanished.

"What? What are you talking about? I don't want you to fail. I want you to be successful and happy, and I want us to be out there and let people see that we love each other."

"Well, that's not reality. You're living in some strange land that has nothing to do with the world," Carla got out of bed and walked away. I got right out of bed and followed her.

"And the illusion of a life you're living is just that, Carla, an illusion. Tell me, what does pretending and lying have to do with living in the real world?"

She turned around quickly and pushed me up against the wall, kissing me. I felt her tears on my cheek. I wrapped my arms around her waist and caressed her head, held her.

"It's okay," I said. "You're not going to lose anything. I won't tell anyone, and I'll pretend we aren't —"

I didn't want her to feel forced to choose between her career and me, but secretly, or selfishly, I wanted to be chosen. She chose her film partner, her manager, her work, apartment, her city, and I was her girlfriend. I had chosen and fallen for her, intoxicated by discovery, touch, companionship. I wanted to believe in love. I wanted her to love me enough that she could choose me like she chose everything else and have it be known, be public. I wanted to be out.

# CHAPTER
# TWENTY-NINE

CARLA WAS DRINKING more and wouldn't sleep with me unless she was drunk. A few days after our conversation about being out we were on her black leather couch in her new apartment, holding each other and kissing. She pushed me down on the couch slowly, and while lying on top of me, she brought her lips close to my ear and whispered, "We're going to go to hell for this."

I sat up, uncertain that I had heard her correctly.

"What the fuck did you just say?"

She looked at me as if she had shocked herself, too, with that phrase. "I'm sorry," she said and rubbed her eyes with her hands and covered her face. "I'm sorry. I didn't mean it."

"We're not going to hell, Carla."

"I'm sorry," Carla said again without looking at me. I grabbed her hand and kissed her palm softly. Her eyes moved up to meet mine. "But why choose this, right?"

"I like who we are."

"Do you think you are ... because of what your mother did?" she asked, so calmly.

"No, that's sick." I was about to get up. The question was possibly innocent, but felt like judgment, like a hidden thought she had, and I wanted her to take it back. But Carla kept going, lost in her own reality.

"I just, I don't want to be like my mother," Carla said. She rarely mentioned her mother.

"Come here." I opened my arms. She curled up inside my arms like a child, with her face resting against my chest, vulnerable as a baby bird, her skin soft against mine.

"My mother was a lesbian, but she didn't do anything with her partner. They would read the Bible every night together instead of having sex. They thought they were sinners, but they loved each other and lived together for fifteen years like that, fighting, praying."

"You never told me that. That's just … sad. I don't want to be like your mom or her girlfriend. And we're not sinners."

Carla's lips came up to meet mine and we kissed softly. It felt like goodbye.

How time changed things.

When I needed Carla, she was there. Even the worst days with her were better than all the lonely days without her. Even the days when I was starving or mean or struggling with flashbacks, she made me feel loved, told me things I needed to hear. "I won't let you drown, Jojo. Shush, it's okay," she'd say while she rocked me on my bed for comfort. And she didn't let me drown. And we laughed. We laughed and laughed when, drunk, we missed our mouths with cups. We laughed together at dialogue in movies and cried together in the cinema, staying in our seats long after all the other moviegoers had left, while young employees swept popcorn around our feet. And we never stopped loving poetry or making up characters for our imagined movies. We talked about getting old, how she would paint and I would write, or we would move to Florida and have a food stand by the ocean.

Carla showed up in my darkest moments when no one else would, and no one could see just how special she really was. But it was in the light, in public, where that tenderness and support faded, where she became a stranger. It was our undoing.

# CHAPTER THIRTY

"HEY, CARLA."

I ran to where other people were greeting her at her film opening at the Uptown Theatre on Yonge Street. She looked beautiful in a pantsuit, jacket, and new boots. I'd even dressed up, worn a blazer and shirt and shined my shoes. I wanted to give her a big squeeze. It was thrilling to be at the Uptown with her.

"Hey." She gave me a quick hug, then whispered in my ear, "You need to sit in the middle of the theatre. You can't sit with us." She pulled away from me, smiling. "Hope you like the show." She walked away to join her film partner in the first row of seats.

I looked around and saw familiar faces from the film industry. My heart was racing. Why hadn't we discussed this?

People waved or smiled in recognition, took their seats, so I had to take mine, relegated to the role of acquaintance, not allowed to sit with Carla on the opening night of her movie, but among strangers in the middle. All I could think of was having to pretend Carla and I weren't lovers, that we didn't read together, drink, laugh, sleep, or spend our nights together. It took everything in me to force a smile, to clap and cheer, to pretend as I stood at a safe distance while people shook her hand at the end of the movie, as fans and peers offered congratulations, hugs and kisses. She didn't look at me as I stood near the concession stand, as I watched life happen around us, as if the movie hadn't ended and the projector was still running. This was indeed fictional and required my best acting.

I finally found my courage, squashed the dragons out of my belly and made my way to where she stood with her film partner as people trickled out of the theatre. She smiled at me and introduced me to a small group gathered around her.

"Do you know Joanne Vannicola? She's a great young actress, was in one of my films."

I smiled again, feeling just that much more uncomfortable, barely able to keep the bile out of my throat. *No, actually, I'm your girlfriend, your lover.*

"Hi, nice to meet you." With a forced smile, I shook the hands of strangers. "Well, I just wanted to say that I loved the film ... and, um ... well, I guess I'm going to be going," I said.

"Thanks for coming," Carla responded.

I didn't leave right away, but slowly walked toward the washroom. Several minutes later, I came out with very clean hands to find Carla still had a group around her. I walked past and waved goodbye. She didn't wave back.

I dashed out of the building and walked and walked as the clock pushed past 10:00 p.m., then 11:00. I calculated the distance between Carla and me, the age gap large enough for a whole lifetime to pass, fifteen years. I had left home around that age.

Perhaps it was my fault, not standing with her, taking up space, but I knew not to. It was like a gay code one shouldn't break.

I went into a coffee shop and sat looking out through the glass window onto Yonge Street, where people walked back and forth, holding hands, talking, or were simply alone. I finally understood that it had nothing to do with me; it was about her. Though I wanted to believe she would come out and that I would be enough for her, I wasn't. I knew I would never bury my truth again — wouldn't allow myself to hide, even if the price was high, even if it cost me my own career. How many times had I hid behind some mask of makeup in an audition room? Or tried to cover up being lesbian to please the men who sat behind tables, with stone expressions or eyeballs too wide for their faces, staring at places below my neck as I recited lines from scripts, wondering if they would hire me? They perused my resumé after my chest, legs, and hips, undressing me with their eyes, projecting their likes or dislikes so obviously, smiling or distant, or unimpressed. Stone.

*Do you mind pulling up your pant bottoms and unbuttoning a few buttons of your shirt?*

*Yes, I do mind.*

Once in a while there was magic, a moment when a director was excited because I gave a solid performance, but those moments were rare. Acting was like heroin, chasing the first high, the best role, the applause, but I wanted something real, wanted more.

I had met Carla in one of those rooms, but I didn't think of what happened between us in the same way because she wasn't a man, and because we both lived in a misogynist and homophobic culture. Even with the power imbalance between us, I thought what we had was special, maybe because she was my first female partner. Perhaps it was special, but it was doomed. I was finally ready to be out because of love, but Carla wasn't.

I fished out my watch from my pocket, the old-fashioned kind dangling from the end of a long silver chain attached to my belt. It was late. The streets were bare, with few people walking by. The sky was dark blue, almost black. A man tapped my shoulder. "Can you spare some change?"

He had lines marking his entire face, a grey beard and hair, saggy dirty pants, and gentle eyes. His fingers were long and thin and marked by age. I stood and gave him what I had left in my pockets. He looked at me and I saw how any one of us could be him. I was afraid of losing everything, but understood that some things were out of my control.

I left the café having made a decision. I was going to break up with Carla.

# CHAPTER
# THIRTY-ONE

"NO ONE'S EVER going to love you like I do."

Carla was angry.

I was walking behind her on Parliament Street after we exited the Irish pub. It was a couple of days after her film's release. I had tried to let her enjoy that first, before we saw each other again.

"Maybe it's true.... I don't know, Carla.... Don't be mad. Don't —"

"Look, do what you gotta do. I'm not going to stick around if your mind is made up ... but I love you and you're making a mistake." She looked at me, but I didn't know what to say. "Fuck it." She stopped walking and looked back at me. "I love you, okay? I would have loved you for a long time. I wasn't asking for much."

"Okay," I said back. I was so stupid, such a child, couldn't even figure out how to answer, how to give a response like *Being closeted is too much*.

"I'm sorry," I said.

"Yeah, me too. Bye, Joanne."

"Bye."

# CHAPTER
# THIRTY-TWO

IT WAS THE WINTER of 1989. I was in my studio watching the evening news in the dark. It was horribly cold and snowy. Injured from a fall a few days after breaking up with Carla, I was lying on my couch, doped up on Percocet, when the breaking news hit the screen and images of ambulances and gurneys, sirens and mayhem took over all the programming in the country. It was December 6, the day of the massacre at École Polytechnique in Montreal: the deadliest mass shooting in Canada's history. Many were shot, and fourteen women were killed.

M.L. called them "feminists," gunned them down after separating them from the boys. As the news of the dead and injured continued into the night, her name suddenly flashed across the screen: Geneviève Bergeron.

The night slowed and the moment was memorialized as one young woman after another was transported from inside the school on gurneys. Footage flashed across the screen with bodies covered up, cameras, the whirl of sirens, screaming bystanders, crying family members. I didn't know what to do, but all I could think about was my friend Marc. He and Geneviève had been girlfriend and boyfriend for five years. I last saw them laughing in the theatre in Montreal, with their beat box, holding hands, teens in love.

I picked up the phone to call him. His mother answered, and I heard his grief in the background. "He's on the bed with his teddy bear," she said, heartbroken. "He can't come to the phone."

"Tell him I love him, I'm so sorry. Wrap your arms around him for me."

I spoke with a couple of friends from my old theatre company in Montreal during the night. A private pain turned into a public outcry, a public moment of shame and anger over the loss of so many young female lives.

It unhinged me. Something came undone, fell away; the dream of life in the world getting better for girls was wiped away in a heartbeat. I wanted to believe in the goodness of people, that all would wake up one day and want to end oppression. Why would people not want equity for their daughters and mothers? It seemed like a no-brainer. The world was not safe. I knew that already. But girls were getting shot, and Geneviève was dead.

The culture was broken.

There were many of us who knew those fourteen young women — hundreds — and then thousands who knew the hundreds, and millions around the world who were touched by this moment of grief, this act of terrorism. I didn't know why men hated women so much, or why people hated gays or black people or Indigenous people. Humanity confused me. I wanted life to be about love. Maybe love ran alongside life, and if you were lucky the lines would cross and you would experience love. But I understood that there was very little that was humane about us. We were a violent species. We were flawed and constantly digging ourselves out of the wreckage.

# CHAPTER
# THIRTY-THREE

IT WAS THE MIDDLE of winter when I descended into darkness.

It was so cold outside and the view was always the same: naked tree branches, snow lining the buildings and streets. Frost and ice collected inside the window sills, fogging up the glass. A deep fog had taken over my body as well. I had no family, I was out of work, I was still struggling over the shooting, and Carla was gone.

I walked to the washroom, opened the cabinet, then turned the tap on in the sink and splashed water all over my face. I grabbed the cold white porcelain and stared into the drain, hearing the words in my head, the message growing stronger and stronger. *Do it.* I felt like there was a layer of gauze wrapped around my entire body, unravelling, exposing old wounds.

I lifted my face to the mirror. Indifference clouded my senses, taking over as if I had swallowed a handful of pills. The quiet held the ghosts of my past, and my mother's eyes were nearly visible in the reflection in the mirror behind me.

I screamed, then started to kick the wall. I kicked and shouted. I pulled the shower curtain down and put a hole in the wall with my foot while I continued to scream. I opened the cabinet above the sink and threw the contents onto the ground, then grabbed the thin glass shelf that held the bottles and soaps, pulled it out of the cabinet, and smashed it on the floor.

Sweat mixed with tears, my heart beat quickly as the rage lifted and I fell to the floor in exhaustion. I looked at the broken glass beneath my body, small shards all around, and I grabbed a piece and felt its sharp edges with my fingertip. I started to slowly cut into my wrist, drawing a tiny amount of blood.

"Oh shit." I stood up and turned on the tap, stuck my hand under the stream. The air was thin as my limbs started to shake. I put a bandage on and made my way outside, where everything seemed upside down, clouds beneath my feet and my head in the ground, suffocating. I hopped on a streetcar and decided, without thinking, to go see Alice. There was no place else to go.

Alice sat in her chair while I was curled up on the floor holding my legs, words falling from my mouth. I'd showed up unannounced, frantic. I'd already told her about the break-up with Carla, before I fell on my back and ended up at home on painkillers. But I didn't know how to stop the downward spiral. I searched for the wolf in her eyes, but never saw it. I dropped my head down again, faced the floor, words desperate to come out.

Alice looked at me without speaking, waiting for me. I had been carrying around this horrible question I didn't know what to do with.

"Carla asked me if I thought I was a lesbian 'cause my mother sexually abused me."

"What did you say back?" Alice asked.

"I said no." I looked again at Alice, wondering if she might hate me, if she would think there was something wrong with me.

"You don't think I'm a lesbian because of what my mom did to me, do you?" I didn't know what she thought, but I was afraid that when she looked at me, she saw something horrible.

"No, I don't think that. What do you think?" she asked.

"I think I'm a lesbian because it's who I am, because I like women. I think I've always been like this, but Carla ... it was like she brought my mother right into the room with us and I couldn't see Carla sometimes, just my mother, and I don't want my mother to be in my relationships with me. I want to get her out. I was a kid and she was my mom and I didn't turn into a lesbian because of her ... and anyway, it doesn't make sense. Wouldn't girls turn straight and want guys if women molested them, if they didn't want to be reminded of their abuse?" Then I laughed and imagined how many lesbians there would be roaming the planet if it were true, because men had raped women in the millions. "But asking me that is like asking straight women if they are straight because they were abused by their fathers. Why ask me that about my mother? It's gross."

"Do you think you saw your mother in her because of the age difference?" Alice asked.

"No, it was more like shame. We couldn't tell anyone. I told Carla I didn't feel bad for being a lesbian."

"Do you think she does?"

"Yes, I think so. But I can't hate being a lesbian. I don't want to hide and I don't want to think about my mother in this way ..." I'd never had a conversation like this.

"You don't have to," Alice said. "Do you think people are who they are inside no matter what others do to them?"

I nodded yes while I picked at my jeans, still looking down. "My mom was crazy. I mean, she was smart and sometimes she was funny and people really liked her, but at home ... at home she did things no one would believe, like she did with my dad. She would just make shit up and pretend we did something wrong when we didn't so she could watch him beat us up. She knew he would beat us. He was vicious."

"I'm sorry."

"I was out at a bar with Martha and she told me that my mom confided in her …" I stopped speaking.

I dropped my head, chin to the floor, not wanting to look at Alice. I didn't want her to see how ugly I was, how disgusting. And that old inner voice came bubbling up from deep inside, coming awake from a sleep, winding her way through my belly and into my throat: *She won't believe you. No one ever does.*

"What did Martha say?"

"I was afraid to tell you when I met you…. I thought you would think I was lying. I wanted Martha to take it back, so I could pretend I hadn't heard the things she said about my mother …" I stopped talking again.

"It's okay to say. I believe you," Alice said calmly.

She waited for me to speak. I saw her shift in her chair slightly.

"I was in shock. I was just trying to keep it together. I told Martha I forgave her, but I didn't. I just didn't know what to do. She knew about my mother." I looked at Alice.

What was Martha sorry for all those years ago? For knowing my mother was a pedophile?

"Sorry for what?" I said loudly, punching the floor in front of Alice. "I looked up to her. I trusted Martha. She didn't give a shit about anyone but herself. I did everything I could to get away from my mother. I was dying, Alice. I was starving to death."

*Stop talking, because she won't stay. She'll crack you open, scatter you around in pieces and I'll have to clean up the mess. You have to shut up. Shut up, Joanne!*

I wrapped my arms around my legs, my eyes closing, axis shifting sideways, like time didn't exist, rolled back, back into my house where I had my fort under the porch, back to her, my mother, on her bed or in the bath, larger than life.

"Why didn't anyone stop her?" I asked in a small voice.

*Don't. Don't do it.*

"What did your mother do?" Alice asked.

*Please listen, she'll hate you if she knows. She'll think you're awful, dirty. Stop now.* The voice inside was so loud.

"I didn't understand why my mother wanted to lie down with me. I just felt bad. I felt sick, like I didn't know who she was, like she was a different person, because I didn't recognize her. I didn't understand."

"What do you mean you didn't recognize her?" Alice asked.

"My mom had a blank look in her eyes like I didn't exist, like she was not in there, like she was someone else. It scared me. Please don't … I don't want to … I'm going to be sick, I'm going to be sick. Please make it stop."

"You're okay. You're not there, Joanne. You're here with me in my office and you are safe and no one is going to hurt you. I promise."

My eyes were closed. I had gone back in time. I was five, six, seven, and my mother was exposing herself to me.

"Joanne, can you hear me?"

"Yes. My body, it's numb. I can't —"

Everything was melting inside, everything mixing together. I could feel the skin pulling at the corners of my mouth. The crashing memories were loud, like the volume had been turned to high. I couldn't get any air. I wanted to open my lungs but they were squeezed tight and my mother was trying to choke me.

"Breathe. Breathe in," I heard Alice say, sounding as if she were in another room, far away.

My breath was shallow. I took deep breaths, but I couldn't get enough oxygen. It was like drowning, and I could hear Alice's voice again telling me to breathe, to open my eyes.

"I didn't hurt her. She hurt me. I had to get away from her," I said in a whisper.

"It's not your fault. You were just a girl, and she shouldn't have hurt you. She was your mother."

"But I … I stopped talking to her, and she went away. She left me alone to take care of myself and told everyone how awful I was for shutting her out, like she did everything she could for me and I was the ungrateful daughter and I couldn't do anything right. People just hated me and blamed me for hurting her."

"You were just trying to survive."

"She was the victim, right, the victim of her own children?"

She had taken so much. I thought of my sisters, who had barely made it out.

"I'm sorry," Alice said.

I looked around the office. My breath had calmed down, and the feeling in my limbs had returned. I shook my arms, trying to feel them again. The office came into view — the window, the pictures on her walls, Alice in her chair looking at me with a type of love, empathy, her eyes locked on mine. I crawled over to her chair and put my head on her lap, gently. Her hands were on top of my head, stroking my hair as she said softly, "It's okay."

After a few moments, I wanted to say her name. "Geneviève Bergeron. Did you see the news? He killed her. He killed so many."

For the first time ever, I saw tears forming in Alice's eyes.

"Yes, it's horrible."

I thought girls like Geneviève would always be safe, the loved ones, the ones with mothers and fathers and houses and education. It changed everything when you knew it could be any girl, anytime, anywhere.

"I don't know how to feel safe anymore," I said.

"Just keep fighting. Just take care of you and don't let them win," Alice said. I knew she meant it for herself, too.

"People just die or disappear. They leave."

I stayed there for what seemed like forever, without speaking, until I heard her say it was time to go. I slowly stood, trying to get my balance, the room still spinning.

"Are you okay?" she asked.

"Yeah, I'm okay. Thanks."

"See you next week. If you need me, you can call."

"Okay, see you next week. Thank you, Alice."

I was writing in my notepad in bed that night, with a cigarette dangling from my lips, the pencil tip between my fingers. I thought of my childhood climbing tree, tall, her twisted branches like brains shooting up into the sky, tangled and full. Nothing could topple her highway of branches and leaves because her roots were buried so deep only an earthquake could bring it down. I would be like her: tall and full and mighty. I would try.

# CHAPTER
# THIRTY-FOUR

NEEDING TO SEE women like me, I set out to meet women and lesbians who were taking women's studies and social sciences at George Brown College. I wanted to make sense out of chaos, to find women who did not apologize or hide or make excuses for violence or deny reality. I also needed to heal.

I met women of all shapes and sizes, with short hair, no hair, rings that stretched earlobes; middle-class women in suits and young women like me, in their twenties and busting at the seams with a desire to join the women's revolution. I was naive, but I sought out like-minded comrades.

I was rough around the edges, wore jeans and leathers, took up space. Women were introducing themselves, women from the suburbs who had left husbands and had children, women who had homemaking careers or worked in social services already, and women who were activists, women I'd seen at marches and rallies. Then I met *her*. Her name was Elia. She wore jeans torn at the knees and large black combat boots. Her hair was short and black, and she clanked from all the silver bracelets on her arms.

"… and I'm Spanish. I work at a hostel for homeless women, and I love my job. I love the people I work with … and that's me," Elia said, shrugging her shoulders and smiling.

I couldn't stop looking at her, the way her hands fell on her lap when she finished speaking, the way her head fell to the side when she smiled.

I sat with my legs open in class, not closed together or crossed. Even my inflection and vocal cadence changed, though it wasn't conscious. I wanted to shed parts of myself, be this other woman that no one knew. Becoming her was like trying on a new outfit. When it was my turn to speak, I told everyone I was an actor thinking about a second career. As I spoke, I looked at Elia, who smiled at me.

Elia and I went for drinks, ordered vodka, and kissed for hours — three hours to be precise. No one cared, not even the server who brought us our drinks and occasionally interrupted us to ask if we wanted another screwdriver. At midnight we left the bar and carried on our public displays of affection.

"I love making out with someone with the risk of being seen, caught," Elia said as we continued to kiss in someone's garage off an alley. We were not very conscious of our safety. She hopped up on an old washing machine and stared at me in the dark, and I moved in to kiss her.

"I've never met anyone like you," I whispered between kisses a few days later. Elia and I were at my apartment. She made pasta with wine sauce and wore boxers with an open shirt and her bra exposed. She was older, more experienced with women. I was a little out of my element but didn't want her to feel unwanted or undesired.

Elia sat on my legs, facing me in the chair, her bracelets clacking as she lightly pulled my head back to kiss me again. I brushed her cheek with my palm. Her large brown eyes looked into mine.

"What is it?" I asked.

"I've never been with someone like you."

"What does that mean?" I was nervous.

"You're just sweet, and I don't want to hurt you," she said.

"You're sweet, too."

"I just know it never works out, baby," she said.

"Maybe I'm not who you need. Maybe you need someone older?" I said. Elia was twenty-eight. And while Carla was much older, Elia was more experienced somehow. I tried to make her feel wanted, but inside I was still that little child, learning to ride the bike without training wheels. "Maybe you need someone who is more stable, experienced," I said.

"Maybe we can just be friends … with perks," she responded. I liked that part, the perks.

"But why are you so sad?" I asked.

"I'm not."

I let my face drop so she couldn't see into my eyes anymore. I kissed her neck, then rested my face on her shoulder. "Let's just not describe what we are, maybe? Let's just hang out and see what happens." I lifted my face again to look into her eyes.

She smiled. I ran my hands through her hair and we kissed again. This was more than casual.

"We can do that," she said between kisses.

Through the course of the night, her shirt was buttoned, her jeans covered her boxers, and we sat at the table talking. She was beautiful and confusing. So was I, I suppose.

Our first bottle of wine sat empty on the table, next to an ashtray and dripping wax candle. The second bottle of wine was half full, and we were half drunk. We talked about women, revolution, Spain, and her mother.

"Did she love you?" I asked, while dragging on a cigarette. I wanted to know how other women were mothered. It helped somehow. I wanted to know what it was like, emotional safety, if I could imitate the feeling, soak it up.

I was in my apartment working on a paper for school a few days later when the phone rang.

"You've been nominated for an Emmy," my agent said. "I tried to call you earlier but couldn't reach you."

"Me?" It couldn't be.

"Yes, for *Maggie's Secret*. Congratulations, Joanne."

Al Waxman was nominated, too, as director, as were the very producers who had considered firing me.

After arriving in Hollywood with my tuxedo in bag and no money to my name, I was picked up in a limo and taken to a friend's beachfront apartment in Santa Monica, near the pier. I had the couch for a bed.

In the morning, I walked along the sand and sat under the sun while the gulls and pelicans dived and dipped for fish and other food. The sound of the water mixed with human voices and the singing gulls provided warmth and slowed time. I was excited, preparing for my big night with the television actors, talk-show hosts, news anchors, producers, directors, and all the other stars who came out for the awards. The Emmys were not as popular as the Oscars, but still, it was as exciting as Gay Pride or Christmas. *I am nominated for an Emmy.* It was exhilarating, and though I tried not to be filled with too much pride, I was proud of myself. I had accomplished something unique as a young Canadian lesbian.

My excitement turned to near boredom during the awards, which seemed to go on endlessly. I was seated at a large table surrounded by other tables where the women sat draped in expensive gowns and the men wore suits like me. I was the only woman in a suit, and it was awkward. I was a Canadian woman. Also awkward. No one paid attention to me until my name was called, and when I didn't get up, Al nudged me. "Go, Joanne, go. They said your name."

I'd been clapping without realizing that I'd won.

"Me?"

I hopped up out of my chair and ran to the stage, clumsily got up, and stood before the microphone, where I thanked Al Waxman and the producers and writers and network. Then I was whisked backstage with my Emmy, where a few snapshots were taken. I noticed people smiling and clapping while I was on stage, but I still felt out of place among the grown-up women in gowns — the Susan Luccis of the world. But the rest of the night was celebratory, with dinner in Hollywood, champagne, interviews, and a moment of recognition between Al and me, one of accomplishment and pride.

The following day I flew back to Canada with my Emmy in my luggage, anxious to get back to feminist circles, auditions, cracker-and-peanut-butter meals, my small apartment, and Elia.

Elia wrapped her arms around me as we slow-danced on my living room floor, my Emmy statue on the desk. She had brought over her beat box and tapes. We held each other, slowly turning in circles, kissing.

"My Emmy-winning actress …"

"I'm not just an actress," I said after gently kissing her neck and face.

"Okay, my little butch," Elia said with a laugh.

"Friends with benefits, remember?"

She could have called me anything, and I would have still kissed her slowly as we turned in circles to Spanish love songs.

"*Te deseo.*"

"I'm not sure what that means, but it sounds good."

It was a time of mass protest; post-bathhouse raids; AIDS actions; and legislative decisions around LGBT rights, the right to benefits in common-law relationships, and rights for LGBT people in the workforce. I was filled with all the energy of a youthful protester with a big mouth and always found my way to the streets to stand in solidarity with my brothers and sisters. Eventually, I would give speeches about the right to marry and organize demonstrations, but then I was all guts, a baby dyke in training, a soft butch finding her way in the world outside my career in the arts and in solidarity with my people. I had learned much about the reality of women's lives globally — about bride burning, dowries, religious persecution, foot binding, how the vote for women was won, female genital mutilation, *Roe v. Wade*, two-spirited history, and genocide. I would fight in memory of women killed, and for those of us living.

"We have received a complaint about you both," said the director of the program at George Brown College. Elia and I were taking some courses together and had both been summoned.

"You're kidding, right?" Elia asked as if she already knew why.

"What for?" I asked.

"There was a complaint about your kissing in front of the school."

"Are you serious?" Elia asked.

I didn't say anything. For the first time in my life I had a girlfriend who was demonstrative, who didn't hide her lesbianism and did not care what other people thought. *Fuck them.* I had a right to kiss outside like other young lovers did. Being gay was no longer a crime under the law. If we wanted to kiss, that was our choice. The meeting with the director didn't last long. She knew she had no right to ask us to hide.

"Let's have a kiss-in," Elia said when we were outside again, looking around at all the other students who shared programs with us. "I wonder who the homophobes are?" Elia and I looked for straight couples. Were other people kissing, holding each other? Was someone looking at us with a scowl on his or her face?

"Kiss me now," I said to Elia, making sure we were as close to each other as possible, facing each other on the steps in front of the main doors with our hands reaching out to one another. We kissed as if it were our wedding day.

After a long kiss we walked back inside the school and went to class.

We made it a rule to kiss as often as we could on campus. Other people would just have to deal with it. We hadn't committed any crime, and unless kissing was going to be regulated for all students in love, straight and gay, then we would kiss every chance we had.

# CHAPTER
# THIRTY-FIVE

I HELD ON TO MY SECRETS about my mother in feminist circles. I had to. No one talked about women who hurt women. I didn't want to take away from the larger conversations about sexism, racism, or male violence against women, but when I started to ask or mention the idea of women as perpetrators, I was chastised. It kept me out of the circle, unable to speak to it because the space was needed to talk about misogyny. I understood because I felt the same way, except I needed to be silent once again, even though I wanted to fight the women who screamed at me, and on a few occasions I did.

"It doesn't mean I hate women because they hurt me. I know what it's like to be hurt by men." I wanted to say *It's not my fault*. It wasn't — wasn't my fault that I carried my mother on my back, all the shame she heaped on my shoulders. I apologized for exposing it when I heard things like "It's so rare, there aren't even any stats" or "It's not the same."

I wasn't comparing, and if it was rare, then I was rare but just as real.

But it wasn't healthy to apologize for a history I had no part in making. They could not hold on to my reality while battling sexism; it inspired a rage in others I didn't know what to do with, so I apologized. Women could not let go of their ideas of the struggling mother or the good mother or the abused wife, and the narrative I presented took away from that focus. But people forgot the context — that men and women who grew up in violence or abuse were not immune to repeating the patterns of abuse simply because they might be female. We hadn't been able to get the culture to acknowledge that sexism and male violence were at the core of so many of our struggles as women, so to expose the abusive woman, the abusive mother, was just too much for many. Women may live in a misogynist culture, but so, too, do women have power over those more vulnerable: children. We do no one any good by believing we do not have power, or power over. Just as my mother had been an abused girl, had been victimized by the province she grew up in and the rules of her generation, she, too, had power over her children. All of this was true at the same time.

I couldn't allow myself to feel invisible, not after surviving both my parents, not after the journey to get to where I had arrived. It had been a lifetime of trying to tell. I could not speak when I was a child, could not find words as an adolescent, had nearly died from starvation while trying to tell the world about my mother and my father, and had almost erased my lesbian identity to keep others safe, to not rock the boat, to fit into the industry. It had been a lifetime of secrets. I could not allow my reality to be dismissed in order to protect someone or something else anymore.

Every woman I met carried their experiences in their bodies. It was in every face and story shared, even by the most stoic and brave of women, the toughest women or butches, even those who had killed men or had been in prison, whose armour cracked and who shed tears while recounting the wounds of homophobia, hate, rape. I presented an unusual and complex reality without reference for others, which made it difficult to believe and hold. So I found solace in silence again, the safest space.

Elia and I went our separate ways at the end of the school year. We met for tea one day, and she described herself as a self-saboteur who wanted to be single and date multiple women. She flirted wildly during our goodbye. I would miss her.

I would also miss seeing lesbians who were fierce, intelligent women, who would not try to pass as heterosexual. I finally saw myself reflected in others; it was like arriving home, but I had to leave. I decided to leave everything, even Toronto. I would give my career a shot in California. I had no idea what was waiting for me around the corner, but after getting my driver's licence, I thought I was prepared. Hardly. If Toronto had been misogynist and homophobic, Tinseltown was far more extreme.

# CHAPTER
# THIRTY-SIX

"I KNOW WHO YOU ARE, but you have to wear some lipstick, try a little harder."

I sat in a chair in a brightly lit office in Los Angeles, opposite a beautiful woman — a talent agent. I understood the code, the words she didn't say about my being a lesbian. I wore ripped, faded jeans and a leather jacket. I was, however, wearing makeup and wondered why she hadn't noticed. Even this face-painting effort hadn't won her over.

It was my Hollywood expedition, post–Emmy win. I was on the cover of *Entertainment Weekly*, and according to industry types, was on my way.

"Hang on," she said as she lifted the receiver of the phone on her desk. "Hi, Marcia ... I've got a new actress I want you to meet, a cross between Angelina Jolie and Jodie Foster. Tomorrow?" She smiled at me, nodding. "Perfect. Send the script over and I'll give it to her before she leaves ... Joanne Vannicola. Okay, talk later." She hung up. "Okay, tomorrow you are going to 20th Century studios for an audition I lined up. Call me, and stay close to a phone so you can check in. And check your voice mail often."

We walked out of her office and into a room where the script was being printed off for me, complete with binders and notes. This was not Toronto.

"I'll be calling you in a couple of hours after you settle. Where are you at again?"

"Oh … it's near muscle beach, Santa Monica."

"Be prepared to drive a lot."

She ushered me through the reception area, where posters from her clients' movies — Wesley Snipes and others — were hung, and out double doors the size of walls. I nervously said goodbye and made my way to the rental car, clutching my folder.

Driving out of the traffic of Hollywood to the ocean was a great way to escape. At night I would rent a bicycle to ride along the paths, wearing my helmet and long pants — the perfect Canadian, safety first — as I pedalled along the concrete pathways of the pier. I rode the Ferris wheel, trying to figure out why I wanted to be an actor, and wondered how I would fit my feminist lesbian identity into this mix.

Auditions piled up. Every day there were scene pages and scripts and calls from the agent. The other women in the waiting rooms were feminine, beautiful actors sizing me up. Everyone checked each other out, sideways looks and ears wide open trying to hear the others practising. Fierce competitors.

After three days I started having panic attacks. I tried to put on more makeup, bright red lipstick to go with my jeans and tees, but it didn't make much of a difference. I still stood out, and not in the way that Hollywood embraced. I was auditioning for a movie being directed by Oliver Stone and couldn't find myself in the characters I was asked to read for. Not that actors needed to find themselves, but I was so far from the characters in every way that I should have just auditioned for boy parts, might have had more luck. I cried my way to the car, didn't know what to say to the

agent in LA. I didn't have the language for what I was experiencing
— a reaction to homophobic undercurrents and extreme sexism,
not just in the town, but also in the scripts. Everywhere.

"I was nervous. The giant billboards of Marilyn Monroe in the
studios and old famous movie stars ... it got to me," I said to my
agent on the phone, trying to give her a reason for choking at my
last audition.

"That's interesting," she said.

What did that mean, *interesting*?

I hopped in my car on a Friday and didn't call her. I bought a
map and charted my route to San Francisco. I left, driving through
Big Sur and Monterey, looking at sea lions and otters and touching
the earth, seeing pelicans and gulls and a large pod of dolphins off
a tourist boat meant for whale watching. Hundreds of dolphins
chased the boat with such joy. For the first time in California, I
had fun, away from women in heels and with implants and men
with cameras and wandering eyeballs. The natural world could
cure my panic, keeping me in the moment without thinking back
into the past or too far ahead into the future. The natural world
demanded I stay present so I wouldn't miss one second as the dolphins jumped into the air and kept pace with the boat. I never felt
a stronger love than when I was with animals or in nature.

I was running away from LA, and I found the nearest
Goodwill, where I bought a pair of male slacks. I cut my hair and
contemplated a tattoo, but didn't know what to brand myself with.
A dolphin? A turtle? A woman symbol? I finally decided against it.

The ride along the Pacific Coast Highway was good medicine.
I was going to San Francisco, to Osentos, a women's bathhouse
where I'd sit in hot tubs with women like me. When I got there, I
saw women with pixie cuts and eyeglasses, women with big breasts
and little ones, with bellies that hung out over their pubic hair,
women who seemed at home in their bodies. I sat in an outdoor

sauna the size of a mini-trailer for two, with showers, under the stars and fenced in with vines and leaves. Women spoke to each other in loving ways and held hands or lay on the floor inside, meditating on mats and filling their lungs.

There were bars with poetry readings and gatherings of gay people openly displaying affection for each other on the sidewalks and in the markets of the Castro District and beyond. I ate and thought about more important things than self-obsession or judgment of bodies or the definition of feminine. There was art, politics, activism. This was the home of Harvey Milk, of my LGBT ancestors.

Standing outside a gallery a few blocks from my motel room, I saw eulogies in one-by-one-foot square patches for the AIDS quilt. I checked my messages and heard a frantic voice mail, so I called from the pay phone across the street from the gallery.

"Where are you? I've been looking for you. No one knew where you were," the LA agent said to me.

"I'm sorry. Didn't mean to disappear, just needed to get away," I said, not knowing how to tell her how trivial and small it all seemed in comparison to the thousands of messages to the dead on the quilt.

"You can't just take off to San Francisco when there are auditions happening. You didn't even leave a phone number where you could be reached!"

That was on purpose.

"I know, sorry. I'll call you when I'm back." I hung up before she could carry on, gathered my backpack and notepad, and went to the nearest café. Before returning to my room, I stopped by the gallery again, and the AIDS quilt:

*Sister X, died 1988.*

*James from Akron, died age 29.*

*Keith, he walked through our lives.*

*In memory of all the teens who died of AIDS.*

There were patches with images of Betty Boop, Mickey Mouse, hand-drawn hands and rainbows; messages from lovers and friends and family — "You will live on in our hearts" and "Gone too young."

Awakenings arrived at different times, and this was one of them. I knew I could not choose LA. There were no reflections of my people there. They may have wanted the Emmy Award–winning girl they saw in a show, but they didn't want the young woman they saw before them. They didn't want me. I was ahead of my time, culturally, and there was no space for queers.

No matter how hard it was to be a lesbian or a woman in the film business, it was not harder than the lives of children everywhere dying from war, famine, hunger, drought, or AIDS. But it was my life, and while the path would be difficult, I would have to find my way with determination, like many before me. No matter how hard the struggle for equity, I would take the harder route.

I flew home.

# CHAPTER
# THIRTY-SEVEN

I WENT AWAY to a cabin near Bancroft, a few hours north of Toronto. The lake swished against the rocks. I swam close enough to the loons that I could see their dotted feathers and watch them dunk below the surface of the water. It took an hour to inch myself closer to a pair not far from an island in the middle of the lake where their nest of eggs lay waiting. My canoe was resting on the rocks, tied to an old tree with torn-up roots. The tree had fallen on its side, creating a wall that stood ten feet high.

Raindrops started to fall, slowly hitting the surface of the lake until the individual drops turned into sheets of rain ripping and dancing on the face of the water. The loons knew to get out, and they called out the melancholy sound that only loons make. I pulled myself out of the water, too, and took shelter under the canoe, tipping it over and leaning it against the tree for support, climbing under it to wait out the storm before I could paddle back to shore. The sky darkened and there was a huge crack of thunder as lightning lit up the clouds. I was mesmerized by the fury of the storm and by the deep musky smell that rose from the earth as the water pelted it.

When the sky began to clear again, I crept out from under the canoe and opened my mouth to catch the drops on my tongue. Clouds shifted in the wind, the birds emerged from the leafy tree-tops, and the light of the sun rebounded off the lake. I opened my pack and fed myself — carrots and dip, nuts — and drank some water. I ate just enough to give me the energy needed to paddle back to shore, something I would never have done so many years before. I would have paddled on air with nothing in me.

I could have died, was glad I hadn't. Dying was for those whose time had come, who didn't have it in them to live another day, or whose lives were taken by others.

People thought of me as a horrible daughter who had abandoned her own mother. And the anti-violence movement was hard for me to be in because I didn't know how to convince large groups that child abuse can happen from people of either gender, that it was not just fathers.

It was my mother.

No one knew the depth of her obsession with me, how little of me existed when in her shadow, how she tried to live my life for me as if she literally could crawl into my body and make it hers. She tried, and the only thing I could do was to get as far away from her as possible. I couldn't explain it, and couldn't imagine seeing her ever again. I wasn't sure how I would cope when the day came that she would die, but I decided I wouldn't see her, that I would just say goodbye in my own way. It would probably be the only way to manage so I wouldn't lose myself. I had just come to know who I was, was just accepting all of me — actor, lesbian, activist. I wanted more, knew there was more, but had always been defined by other people. I needed to allow myself to exist on my own terms — through feminism, the rise of the LGBT rights movements, social dialogue, marches, sit-ins, and finding ways outside of the characters I played as an actor, learning to know who I was. Maybe I would be an activist or a healer, or maybe even a writer someday; maybe people would understand, but for now what I needed was myself.

A chipmunk appeared in front of me. I threw it a nut from my bag. It approached me and then bit my baby toe, running away when I screeched in surprise and laughed. *Does a baby toe look like a nut to a chipmunk?* I threw the remaining nuts onto the soil and prepared the canoe for the short journey back to the cabin. I had an audition the following day with the famous Québécois filmmaker Denys Arcand, and the character was lesbian. I was nervous, but for the first time in a long time my body felt like my own. I wasn't sure if I would mature into the craft well or not. Maybe acting was like opera or wine. I hoped to one day be able to walk into an audition and not bring every problem of my life, and just be. Just be.

I sat inside a room in the same building where I had fallen in love with Carla, where I sang to her that night with the Pretenders blaring from the speakers. I laughed at the irony of auditioning for a part as a lesbian in this very room, which had now been converted into a more formal space with tables and chairs, though the windows were uncovered, revealing the trees, bushes, flowers, and small waterfall of the large gardens in the background.

Monsieur Arcand had an ease about him and a smile that never left his face — likeable, friendly. It was an omen.

Instead of trying to charm him, I banged a metaphorical gavel in a rant filled with everything I ever wanted to say about the film business and the men who worked in it — the sexist men, the lack of roles for women, the homophobia, and the impact on gay people.

Deirdre Bowen, the casting agent who sat with us, was aghast.

"There are no parts for women. We are supposed to want to hang off the arms of men and starve ourselves to near death, for what? The role of the no-name girlfriend or the prostitute? Really?" I sat up tall while M. Arcand engaged me with an "Ah yes, of course."

"And another thing ... why are there more and more roles with women taking their clothes off? I'm not one of those women."

I rambled while Deirdre seemed to turn a different shade of white, forcing a smile so as not to kill me. I could see she wanted to shut me up, but there was no stopping me.

"There's no reason girls and women should take off their clothes in movies. How does it advance a story? Tell me!"

*Big mouth.* Keeping an acting career was going to be hard.

Denys smiled, nodded.

He hired me anyway, and I took off my clothes anyway.

"You know, Deirdre was appalled and apologized profusely for your rant," Denys giggled. "She said, 'But I assure you she's a good actress.' And I said to Deirdre, 'I'm pretty sure of it. I'll take her,' and that was it, you got the part. You do know that most other women would be throwing themselves at me for a chance to be in my movie, but not you."

And just like with Al Waxman and the arguments around gender and work that led to an Emmy nomination, I would be nominated for a Genie for *Love and Human Remains*, as would Denys. Maybe these gender arguments were working after all? No. It was just sheer luck coupled with hard work, and in spite of my very big mouth.

Miracles did happen sometimes.

# CHAPTER THIRTY-EIGHT

MY TORONTO INTERNATIONAL Film Festival debut was in 1993 with Denys. We arrived at the Elgin Theatre arm in arm. I was dressed in a white shirt and black tie, tailored black tuxedo jacket with tails, finished off with suspenders and shiny new black shoes — perfect butch attire. I'd prepared for the evening only hours before, anxiously wondering how the film would be received. It was, after all, my first love scene, and the first movie in which I'd ever taken off all my clothes.

That day on the set many months back, I had sat for the makeup artist, or stood, depending on which part of my body she was applying foundation to, having decided a layer of foundation would help me feel like I had a second skin while naked on set. I looked like a fool standing on a tall, cushy black makeup chair, trying to balance like a surfer so it wouldn't swivel and bending slightly as the makeup was applied to crevices and areas of my body that no one had seen from those angles before. To say that I was embarrassed was an understatement, but I bent over and pretended that she was merely applying a layer to my arm or neck, not the inside of my butt cheeks or close to my vagina.

At the theatre, we waved from inside the limo at fans lining the streets, their tickets in hand to see our film. Denys was always suave, charming, and level-headed. He had been through these openings many times, been nominated for Academy Awards, won Genies, and received accolades for years. He was a seasoned professional, humble. I truly loved him, which wasn't something I would say about most male film directors.

"Joanne, you look like a boy. A nicely dressed and beautiful boy," he said when he saw my outfit. He giggled, as he often did. We giggled together endlessly like schoolchildren.

I was grateful to find a director who was more interested in my friendship than in sleeping with me, though we were both hopeless flirts, adoring the safety of our secrets, our well-placed boundaries. I was a lesbian after all, and this was my big coming-out role; playing a lesbian for the first time and opening the Toronto International Film Festival really felt like a giant coming-out event.

"Why are you so nervous, Joanne?" Denys asked.

"I've never had a film opening … and I'm just … I take my clothes off, if you don't remember."

"Of course I remember." He smirked.

Before we filmed that love scene, I had put on my robe and drunk a glass of vodka at seven in the morning. I flipped my robe off and kept it off, with my layer of makeup as a substitute for clothes. I convinced myself that this was some sort of rite of passage, just something I told myself to make it through the day. It wasn't a rite of passage as a female actor. That was simply a myth. It wasn't a bat mitzvah or a master's degree — just plain old nudity with a camera.

"Okay, here we are. Smile and enjoy it, Joanne." Denys stood outside the car door, lending me his arm. I climbed out in my flat-heeled leather shoes, tuxedo, and tie, and smiled and waved as photographers snapped pictures. We squiggled some autographs and entered the theatre. This was the most exciting and important time in my career, and it was such a prestigious evening, opening the festival. The occasion was something that would change my life forever, and not necessarily for the good, but nonetheless monumental.

It was the 1990s. South Africa was still under apartheid law. AIDS was still seen as a gay disease. Bill Clinton was the president of the United States. The twin towers of New York were still standing. And there were no lesbian role models in film and television — not even Ellen DeGeneres had come out yet — so playing a lesbian in a large movie with such publicity and with such a grand entrance really did feel like a massive coming out, a moment, like a shift in time.

It was.

"What's it like to play the part of a lesbian? How did you prepare for it?" a woman who sat at the round table at the after-party asked me. I was sitting with one of the leads in the film, who knew I was a lesbian, and she squeezed my leg under the table in a show of support.

"Why? It's not like playing a killer or someone with an accent. It's just like playing any role, or … it's human, nothing to prep for …"

I was anxious, uncertain what her intention was.

"I mean, surely you had to get inside the mind of a lesbian, think about how to do a love scene … and … well, it is different."

I stood up, wiped my mouth with my napkin. "I didn't look at who she is as any different than who I am, if that makes sense." I wasn't certain if her question was a negative or positive one, but I wanted to leave it where it was. I had never heard anyone ask what it was like to play a heterosexual, so I was thrown slightly. Also, she did not know I was a lesbian, but she may have felt embarrassed to ask, had she known, because it would have been a foolish question. It would have seemed foolish if I had asked her as a straight person what it was like to play a straight person. It was likely an innocent question that came from a place of ignorance, or possibly she was fishing to know more about me, but it stuck with me.

It felt good to play a queer character. Even though she was not the most stable character, it didn't matter. She was a lesbian, and this was my moment.

I didn't know how to have the conversation yet about playing a lesbian; it was too close. I wanted to, but didn't have the confidence to speak to what I was feeling, thinking, what life had been, what constantly pretending to be straight in films and television was like — it was erasure. Non-existence.

I wish I'd had the poise to say then that I was a lesbian and that it felt great to play one, to step into the shoes I was born for, to be authentic in film, to be realized, to not hide. And to explain why playing a lesbian was the same as playing a straight person, except I didn't have to change my own identity to play the character, I didn't have to take part of my soul and bury it in order to be who they needed me to be.

I *am* a lesbian. I *want* to play queer roles. I want there to be more and more of them so that I never have to pretend, lie, or hide again, so that I can work and live with dignity and stop the cycle of poverty that queer artists like me are always navigating. Wouldn't it be lovely to not struggle so hard because of who you are?

"Playing a lesbian is just right for this movie. I was happy to step into her skin. Thanks for asking. Excuse me, I have to use the washroom," I said before walking away.

In 1995 I would play my last heterosexual part, in a television movie called *Derby* — the cheesiest flick, but fulfilling. I was the lead, playing a horse-loving girl who would ride in the Kentucky Derby and win to save her family farm — like a TV version of Elizabeth Taylor in *National Velvet*. It would be the last time I would try to pass. I believed I was destined for something more.

I would have another six years to figure myself out, to fall, rise, make mistakes, reflect, rebel, march, speak out about LGBT equity rights. I would have another six years to grow before I would receive the call that my mother had cancer.

In 2000, I had contemplated contacting my mother. I didn't know why my gut was at odds with my mind, as if my gut was drumming something up that went against my own rational thinking and decision-making. I was set on never talking with my mother again. But some deeper part of me must have known something was on the horizon. I just didn't know how to make sense of it until the call finally came: stage four uterine cancer. Terminal.

# The Stories Our Bodies Tell

## PART FOUR

# CHAPTER THIRTY-NINE

2002 — Princess Margaret Hospital

THE DOCTOR TELLS US our mother only has a few days to a week left to live. She slips in and out of consciousness, sometimes fully lucid, present, and able to engage in full conversations, and at other times it's as if we aren't even in the room, like she can't see us at all.

Sadie arrives in Toronto. All four of my mother's children are in the same city for the first time since childhood. We are like teenagers, wanting to bust out of the formality, to ditch the trail of chains attached to us and run and scream, but we don't. We steal away moments when we can let down our guard, my sisters and I giggling like girls, like when we watched television alone in our basement while our parents were away, aware that any moment they could come home. Even now that I am a grown woman in my thirties, my spine tingles like it did every time I heard Sadie scream. Every sense kicks into overdrive, adrenalin rushing right down to the marrow. Danger. Danger. High alert! Like the red code is on, but it is not. I need to self-talk and remind myself I am grown, or whisper with Lou as we connect in the hospital hallway. "You okay?" we ask, and we nod our heads up and down, but our expressions are filled with dread. It's just how it is.

My mother is bleeding out. Her body expels toxins and excrement and blood. She is in pain, and I hate every second of her suffering.

I run to the fridge before stepping into her room and pull out a Popsicle. She can't eat anymore, but I want her to experience some human pleasure. Simple moments are all that can be enjoyed — music on disc, television, art, photographs, being read to. Diego reads to her on his visits, a sacred exchange between them. He is losing his mother. He loves her. I don't want to interfere with his relationship to her, even though it's hard to understand what he does with the information he has been told about her. The pedophilia. I don't think he believes me. The abuse in our family eroded our relationships, but we are all doing the best we can. Siblings seem to have the hardest time accepting the others' truths. It's hard to imagine a loving mother as someone who could want sex with a daughter or sister's boyfriend, who enjoyed the suffering of her own daughters at the hands of a violent husband. But our mother did. And my brother did not experience the abuse in the same way. Diego loves his mother, and he is losing her.

There isn't much in the hospital to find beauty in, and it requires internal effort to even indulge in the thinking up of beautiful things for my mother, but I am determined to help her die with dignity. It isn't hard to do, to be kind. I'm not sure if I am succeeding, but I try.

I enter her room with the Popsicle, break it in half, and sit at the edge of her bed.

"Hey, you awake?" I ask.

She turns her face toward me, eyes open, alert.

"It's grape." I hold up the stick.

"Thanks." She opens her mouth slightly. Her lips are dry. I hold the stick for her while her hands rest on the bed.

"It's good."

"Can you hold it yourself?"

"Yeah." She lifts her hand and grabs hold of the stick.

I walk around her bed to the table and pop some Mozart into the CD player. I pull out her hand cream and her lip gloss.

"I want to talk to you about something," my mother says, staring at me.

I look at her, blood vessels and bruises exposed through her porcelain skin.

"I had a baby when I was fifteen, a boy," she says in a soft tone.

I sit on her bed, look into her eyes, not wanting her to lose her focus in case she forgets what we are talking about or changes the subject, falling away from reality, which she does too often. *Not now, please.* I turn on her reading lamp below all the machines that monitor her heart, her oxygen.

"Tell me about the baby, Mom."

"A boy," she says calmly, without breaking eye contact.

"What year was he born?"

"In 1955. I remember, I was scared because I knew they wouldn't let me keep him."

"Who wouldn't let you?"

"The nuns, the home, my mother, father … but I wanted my baby. I even named him Luke after my father so they would let me keep him, but they didn't."

I feel her emptiness taking over the room, her longing. It is him. Luke takes over the space as if there is an invisible umbilical cord stretching out from her body into the universe, still attached.

I grab the Popsicle stick from her hand as the juice melts onto her blanket.

"You were in a home?"

"Yes."

"Where was it?"

"It was on Stanley Street in Montreal. I remember we used to have to stay inside, hide our bumps ... weren't allowed outside much. They didn't want people staring. We had to keep the curtains shut in the bedrooms, too. Like a prison."

I had learned about these homes of the 1950s from other women, but I had no idea my mother was forced into one.

"Who was the baby's dad?" I ask.

"It was my father," she says, without missing a beat, as if she were talking about the weather. I swallow and ask the same question differently.

"Are you saying that the father of your first-born baby was your own father?"

"Yes."

We stare at each other in silence before she speaks again.

"Do you believe me?" Her expression shifts; she needs to be believed.

"Yes, of course I do," I say.

"Isn't that something, that of all people you believe me? My sisters didn't."

"It's the one thing that actually makes sense to me."

Siblings don't always know these things. They can't always know the truth. Families are tricky.

My grandfather raped my mother. He gave her a baby, then took it away. How many parts of a girl could a father take? How are mothers supposed to be good mothers when all they know is violence?

"I'm sorry," I say.

I can't stop the empathy in me, though I want to. For so many months I tried not to care, as if caring would wipe away my truth. But it doesn't. And I do care. I want to detach, but she is still my mother, and the wall dissipates as she tells me about her son. It is nearly impossible to hold everything at the same time — my own childhood memories along with hers — but it's doable. We all have a history.

I think of Lou, of Sadie, of my animals, and of the girls and women I know who are now gone, passed on. I think of their love, the very thing that provides oxygen, that makes the trees grow, the energy that shows up in birds' nests, that turns caterpillars into butterflies, that pumps air into my mother's chest.

Mother stares at me, her expression flat, still. Her baby long gone.

"What day was your son born?" I ask.

"October 27, 1955, at Royal Victoria Hospital. The girls in the room told the head nun of the house that my water broke. It was the middle of the night and I was screaming. One girl in the room with me was crazy, she even said she would take it out with a butcher knife if I wanted her to, then they couldn't take it away from me, but the nurses came and got me and took me away ..."

Mother coughs.

The hospital room is dark, infused with my mother's grief.

"The girls all used to talk about what they would name their babies and they would knit booties and hats. But in the end every single baby was taken."

"I'm sorry."

"I had another baby, Dot. I named her Dot. A girl."

"Two babies? Was it your father? Was he the father as well?" I ask.

"No ... the father was a boy I met at a concert, a French boy."

"What happened to the girl, Mom?"

"I don't know. I don't remember."

"You don't remember?"

"No, I don't. I don't remember, Joanne." Her eyes blink, getting heavier and heavier until they close, while the music continues to play softly in the background. I cover my mouth with my hand while my mother sleeps, her mouth wide open.

A few moments later her eyes pop open. "What did I miss?"

"Nothing, you were sleeping."

"Oh ..." She looks around the room, then her eyes rest on the picture of a waterfall pasted on her wall. "Did you put that up?" she asks, still staring at it.

"Yes."

"Can you pull out my photo album from my drawer?" She points to the table beside her bed. I grab the small album that I had put together for her, which holds pictures of her children, some photographs she has never seen before from movie sets. And there are photos from her own collection: black-and-whites from the 1950s of Studebaker cars and people posing at the St. Lawrence River; babies in christening gowns; the mountains in BC; her last home in the valley with the Nuxalk people and friends, black bears, salmon leaping through the river in spring — a different life than the one she created with her own children.

"How did you end up with a picture of a bear?" I ask.

"They're everywhere in the valley." She turns the page in the album while I hold it up. She points to a picture of Al Waxman and me with a boom microphone in the background. "What is that?" she asks.

"It was *Maggie's Secret*. A movie."

"You did a movie with the King of Kensington?"

"Yeah, he directed the movie. He was good to me, fought for me," I say. "He believed in me."

She flips to another shot on a movie set, points to a picture of me, my back to the camera, facing a massive cliff with a waterfall.

"It's South Africa. It was so beautiful, everything about it ... the colour of the earth, like clay; the wildflowers, pinks, reds and greens; and the animals, roaming wildebeest, giraffe, zebras. I would be in a car and a herd of cows or monkeys would just file by. It was after the fall of apartheid," I say, remembering the people and the stories I was told while I was there, of the Mandelas and the African National Congress, and remembering my secret escapades at night in Cape Town. I found an illegal underground gay bar and danced to music from the seventies, even though it was the nineties, while men in tight suits sniffed poppers and we all knew to be careful. It wasn't only about race, but about our bond as gay people, an international code of brother- and sisterhood. When not on set, I was off meeting people, trying to take it all in and learn as much as I could. Conversations were not frivolous, not about clothing or which celebrity just got married or divorced, but real communication with near strangers. We were engaged about politics, community, oppression, race, about farming and protests, about Nelson and Winnie Mandela, about history and restorative justice, the stuff that made me come alive.

"Look," Mother says after she flips through a few more photographs. She is staring at a black-and-white photograph of Sadie, Lou, Diego, and me as children. As I look at the image of myself as a one-year-old, my thoughts quickly turn to our conversation of babies, of the siblings I never knew about. I can't imagine what it would have been like to be a pregnant girl in the 1950s, sent away by abusive parents to live with punitive nuns in a home for unwed mothers, to give birth to your own father's child. I don't know what to do with this truth, but I feel the need to protect it, to be gentle.

We stare quietly at the photo and Mother looks away, then opens her mouth to speak, her voice hoarse. "I wish I could have ..." She stops speaking, her voice trails off while she holds all four of us in her hand. Her eyes start to close and open again. I take the album from her fingers, close it, and place it on the table beside her, pull her blanket up and turn out the light.

It is too late for wishes.

# CHAPTER FORTY

2002 — Princess Margaret Hospital

MY MOTHER DIES.

The moment comes after many twenty-four-hour shifts with Sadie and Lou on the same schedule and Diego and I on individual time. Sometimes I stay with my sisters. We snap at each other occasionally, and at other times we giggle in the wee hours of the night in the lounge beside our mother's room, passing the time with stale coffee and cards and Krispy Kreme donuts.

Anything can set us off into fits of laughter — the distant sound of someone moaning, or Sadie's face, which she contorts in exaggerated expressions, the ones she made on purpose to make us laugh when we were little girls. Sadie's eyes widen and she sticks her jaw out, then bites down over her lip with her upper teeth as if she has a massive overbite, like a gopher. For whatever reason, it always makes us giggle, but even more while we are stuck in the lounge on a hospital floor filled with the dying. We are impossible.

"What am I?" Sadie asks, imitating the gopher again, sticking both her hands up for paws, bent at the wrists, making sucking sounds at the same time. I leave the lounge while my sisters snort with laughter, trying to shush each other at the same time.

I leave to sleep at home so I can come back to relieve them later. I'm exhausted from our vigil, from the months leading up to it. I do not share the secret conversations I've had with my mother. Not yet. While I sleep, a bright light wakes me up with a message: "It's time." I hear it and I am awakened by the shining light, but it's not the sun; it is a light I see while sleeping. I jump out of bed and am scrambling to put on my clothes when the phone rings. "Get here now. She's dying." I already know and within seconds I am in the car racing to get there, because *it's time*.

Mother gasps. We are all in her room. I hold her hand on one side of the bed. I gently touch her soft bald head and whisper in her ear, "It's okay to go. You can go."

She continues to struggle for air, looking above her.

Sadie starts to cry and whispers across from me. Then Diego steps up as Sadie retreats.

We are letting our mother go. Time falls away. I am five years old and I am on the streets of Pierrefonds playing tag, climbing trees, on the mountain of Montreal, seeing Mother in the audience of the auditorium, in our home, around the kitchen table, and at Christmastime, the holiday she cherished, with trees and tinsel, song and celebration. As she takes her last few breaths, I remember the moments of joy. Time is a thief, a mystery, a mystic. If we are lucky, maybe we will catch a glimpse of her on the way out, touch the spirit of the woman we dreamed of having but never really knew. I want to see that magic, the purity of a soul.

She inhales deeply, like she is trying to breathe through a straw. She gasps, her eyes widen. She seems so engaged with someone or something above her bed. She nods as if in conversation, or in answer to a question. *Yes*. I desperately want to know what she sees, what she is thinking. Who is she responding to? I look above her and try to see who it is my mother is communicating with. I want to be above her, to receive her on the other side and usher her toward a gentler place where there is no more pain, but I can see nothing, can see no one. Only she knows.

Lou stands by the door, terrified, distant, as if she wants to be entirely on the opposite side and out of the room. Diego cries, something he rarely ever does.

Death has been slowly creeping up, and as much as I am prepared and ready for it, it is happening so quickly. I want her to go, to be gone, but not like this, not in this way. But it is the only way.

I touch her face. She breathes, deeply inhales. Pause. Exhale. I wait for her next inhale while holding my breath, in rhythm with hers, but it doesn't come. I breathe in and she is gone.

Maybe on her way up she can see that we are there for her as she crosses to another horizon, and perhaps, like looking through a telescope, she can see us from the top of the room, can see upward and out, the trees, streets, animals, continents, oceans, the endless sky, until the Earth itself is a distant shining light, like the moon from Earth in reverse.

# CHAPTER
# FORTY-ONE

LOU AND I DECIDE we will help the other four people who have agreed to hold my mother's coffin up as pall bearers. We stand on opposite sides at the back of the coffin. When we pick our mother up, Lou lets out an audible sound of distress as we hold over three hundred pounds of her.

"Oh shit." I start to giggle; then Lou giggles. We can't look at each other or we will be in fits, or worse, we might drop the back end of the coffin.

Walking inside the church isn't any better. Lou and I sit side by side on the wooden pew in the dark cathedral filled with lit white candles. A priest stands in white robes, with one altar boy on either side of him. The priest holds a large chain attached to a round silver object. It has smoke coming from it, the smell of incense. He swings it in front of his body while he talks about God and the afterlife. He doesn't know anything about my mother, doesn't even say the names of her daughters, as if we are invisible. Only Diego is mentioned. It doesn't go unnoticed among us girls; Sadie, Lou, and I eyeball each other as if to say *What the fuck?*

"She had her good days and she had her bad days," the priest sings with no emotion and a badly crafted script. I start to giggle again, the sound low and deep like the turning over of an engine; then it grows, and Lou starts to laugh, and then we hear someone not far behind us whispering "Amen," and Lou and I come undone, like little hyenas, suppressing our laughter and bobbling up and down as if we are crying. We cover our mouths with our hands. I am hoping everyone seated behind us thinks we are overcome with grief as our bodies continue to jerk up and down, faces masked.

At the end of the funeral we carry the coffin again, down the aisle, out of the church. Memories and senses take over as I pass by the faces of friends and old family members I haven't seen in years: Mother at a table of family members playing cards; Aunt Connie and her beer; my mother trying to breathe; singing with Lou as children; the women who had graced my life; the sound of tap shoes — a life review and distraction from the faces that stare at me while I hold my mother up. These are the people who did not believe she was raped by her father. I try not to look too closely and continue toward the exit, toward the sun.

I don't wish to be in this repressive Catholic church, an absurd funeral with a male priest who couldn't even say my mother's daughters' first names, who made us invisible. A gothic theatre with the little boys in robes and the priest with the chain and ball of smoke and the cross that dangles from his chest. I envision my mother laughing. I can bet that had she been able to sit beside me at her own funeral, she would have laughed at the silliness of it all.

This funeral is for those extended relatives mostly, but for me, or even my mother, it is pointless.

*Oh, come on now, stop that laughing,* she might say with a smile, suppressing her own giggles.

I think back to one of our last conversations. "Didn't one of your sisters try to kill herself? Why?" I asked her in the hospital room just a few days ago, before she died.

"Yeah, my sister was depressed. She came to see me in the home for unwed mothers when I was pregnant."

"Do you think something bad happened to her when she was a kid? Maybe even while you were in the home? Maybe your dad —"

Mom shushed me when I asked that question, but it was hard to believe nothing happened to the other five girls. But it was possible, and if anyone knew that, I did. Mom was raped, molested by her father.

"You stop now, Joanne. No more questions," Mom said, drifting, fading.

Those were some of our last private words together.

I look around at the faces of relatives I have not seen in a couple of decades and know that my mother is free now. No more pain.

*No more.*

*Sleep now, Mother. It's okay to sleep.*

# CHAPTER
# FORTY-TWO

SADIE, LOU, AND I gather in Mother's apartment to divide her belongings before Sadie and Lou leave Toronto. Diego has already called dibs on what he wants, leaving us to do the work.

"I went off my friggin' diet and I'm smoking again!" Sadie says from the living room, where she is seated in an armchair. "That goddamn funeral and the stupid nicotine patch just wasn't e-friggin-nough to cope with all that."

"Well, you can get back to it when you get home," I say. I try to be supportive, but all I can offer are the stupid words of a little sister. Hundreds of pounds have made their way onto Sadie's frame over the years. A few times she has referred to us — me, Lou, and her — as small, medium, and large. It always made me laugh. Sadie is excited about weight loss and is feeling good, or was until Mother died.

"Gonna have to start all over again," Sadie says while lighting up.

For every meal I skipped through the years, she ate enough for two people, followed with chocolates and candy and cakes, stuffing everything down — pain and desire buried under flesh that contains it all, like our mother, like our mother's mother.

We all have our coping mechanisms.

"Sadie, Jo, look at this. It's totally vintage." Lou is in Mother's closet and pulls out some old clothes she'd kept for decades. "Look at the velvet and fake fur," she says, holding up a black dress my mother made over thirty years ago for herself, a checkered pattern of black flowers and black sheer material, long sleeved, delicate from head to toe, beautiful.

"I want the Princess Di stuff, and Elvis," Sadie says.

I can't argue, even though our mother has already given me the Elvis albums. The only dishes I want are the golden ones that Mother brought back from Italy, but Sadie wants those, too, so we pack them up for her in bubble wrap and paper, delicate hand-crafted dishes with gold-dusted squares. Sadie promises to give them to me when her time comes. Then she starts hiding things in her luggage and I can't figure out why she is doing that, why she feels the need to take small items like photo frames or a tray with a creamer and milk jar. I decide it's not the stuff per se, but that she just can't get enough, like somehow the things will make up for everything else that has been lacking or taken away. I know it will never be enough. No trinket or glassware, photograph or golden creamer will ever fill the emptiness and grief, will ever make up for the torture Sadie endured at the hands of my father or the psychological degradation by our mother.

I am reminded of Sharon Simone, who sued her FBI father for child abuse and was awarded money, both as a form of compensation for the abuse she and her sisters endured and as public recognition. It mattered, made a difference in how they lived in the world after the court case, and after the movie about their lives. I did think about taking my parents to court, too, but I let it go.

I look at the wall of photographs in my mother's apartment. A few of them are old headshots of me that hang in black frames. Mother loved the fantasy of a star for a child. The daughter she thought she loved was the one in movies and TV shows: a one-dimensional image behind a frame that wasn't real, but posed, created from a photographic negative, a filmstrip. I take the head-shots off the wall, put them face down in a box and walk toward the kitchen. I must tell my sisters.

"I have to talk to you guys. I need to tell you something about Helen, something she told me last week." I grab a Corona from the fridge that I stocked with beer and wine. Lou comes out of the closet with Mom's pink dress, the one she wore when I was a girl.

"Oh shit, ha ha, that dress is so ugly!" Sadie inhales smoke and sits in a large brown armchair facing me. Lou also sits with dresses in her arms and on her lap.

"We don't have a lot of time. Can't it wait 'til we finish with the stuff?" Lou asks.

"No, I really need to tell you now."

"Well, go," Lou says, annoyed that I have pulled her away from the dresses and fabrics.

"Mom had a baby. She had a baby boy when she was a teenager."

"*Whaaat?* What did she tell you?" Sadie blurts out as she shifts her frame toward the edge of the seat, back straight, waiting for me.

"She named him Luke, after her father, and … she was in a home for unwed mothers in 1955."

"Who did she say the father was?" Sadie asked right away. "Was it Dad?"

"No." I take a big sip, gulp down the mouthful of beer. "Luke? She named him after the father …" They don't get it, so I decide to come right out with it.

"She told me it was our grandfather. It was her own father."

"No fucking way, that's a fucking lie. She's lying," Sadie says.

"Holy shit," Lou says.

"It's not a lie. She told me it was her father that molested her. They wouldn't let her keep the baby."

"She's lying, that slut. She just made it up 'cause she's a sick bitch!" Sadie gets up to light a fresh cigarette. "I know she was a slut. She slept around on Dad."

"Even if she did sleep with a hundred guys, it doesn't mean that she's lying, Sadie. You don't have to stop hating her to know that once upon a time she was a kid who got hurt."

"Oh, come on!" Sadie says, her rage turning on me.

"Well … it does make sense, Sadie," Lou says. "I mean, Mom wasn't normal. She was cruel as shit and did stuff to Jo and me and —"

"Oh, please," Sadie interrupts and stares at me as if I am a liar.

"Why are you so mad?" I ask her. "It's not that far a stretch. It makes sense to me, and I don't know why anyone would ever make something like that up."

"How long was he screwing her?" Sadie asks. "How do we know anything? How do we even know if Dad is our own dad?" Sadie sits down again. The hairs on my body stand up, wondering if our father fathered all of us.

"There's no fucking way. She's lying. She's lying," Sadie says again.

Lou and I looked at each other. *What if?*

"Are you fucking nuts? You fucking believe that shit?" Sadie stares at me. "She's so full of shit. She would do anything for attention."

The room falls quiet. My body feels like it has no bones to hold it up. I sit down.

"I don't believe it. I think Luke's father is Dad," Sadie says with determination.

Lou cradles a cushion. "We could have a blood test?" she says.

Sadie perks up. "Yeah … we should all have a blood test and see if we are all from Dad!"

"I don't think Dom is my dad," Lou says. "I mean, look at me, I have orange hair, freckles, and I'm white as a ghost compared to you two."

"Oh fuck." Sadie finally giggles. "That's fuckin' true, eh? Ya are a freakin' ghost. Probably some Irishman. *Ha ha.*" We all laugh.

"Possible, right?" Lou says, hopeful.

Sadie tosses a cushion at her while we name nationalities we think we could be: French. Indigenous. A Scot! I think it might be the moment to tell the other part.

"There's something else ... actually, another baby, a girl. Mom said she also had a girl."

Lou and Sadie stare at me in unison. "But it wasn't our grandfather! See? Something normal!" I say.

"Ahhhh ..." Sadie hollers, exasperated by the conversation. "Shut up."

We argue and pack dishes, pictures, books, and games; toss out garbage and continue to debate how many babies, who the fathers are; curse, eat, put on CDs. Somehow the tension and pain metamorphose into a childlike scene. We are girls again, as time stands still and we listen to music. Together again. Sisters.

We may have been broken, but brokenness itself is something that can be held, like gathering the bones and parts of each of us, embracing those parts, protecting them, and hoping to put them back together again. Lou, Sadie, and I have done the best we could. We have made our way to love. Even in the face of despair or in our well-kept secrets, even in our disbelief of the others' experiences or memories, we love one another.

It is possible to love the broken.

# CHAPTER
# FORTY-THREE

MONTHS AFTER MY mother's death, I decide to call Alvin, her doctor in BC. She visited him weekly when she lived in Bella Coola, in the absent years. I don't think he will speak to me or break his therapy code of ethics, but I feel a need to reach out.

I am prepared for the things that come out of his mouth. He talks as if he has been waiting for me to call so he can tell me every-thing. He claims that my mother had fragmented consciousness and didn't always know who she was. He tells me she was sexually and physically abused by both her mother and father. They locked her in a pantry for long periods of time. She was handed to other adults for sexual purposes. She was abused by a man who ran a funeral home beside her house, a mortician who raped her in cof-fins. Her parents threatened that they would cut out her tongue if she told. She couldn't recall abusing her own children, but won-dered if our grandfather had hurt us. He says that my mother had multiple personalities, some with names, with varying character-istics: threatening parts, childlike parts, cruel and angelic. Mother also wondered if our own father had done anything to us sexually. The list goes on and on. The call lasts nearly an hour. I scribble notes, afraid to interrupt in case he might stop saying all he knows, until he finally stops.

"I have boxes of files stored in my basement," he finishes.

"Can I ... can I have those boxes, Alvin? Can I see the files?"

He doesn't answer right away and I can sense he feels he might have said too much, that he wants to protect me, or my mother. "No ... I don't think that will be possible."

"Okay. Thank you, Alvin," I say. We hang up.

Everything seems to fall into place. Even if some of it is questionable, who cares? Hearing about my mother's life, the stories she never told, her fragmentation, the abuse, her history, I have, for the first time, a window into those years, can look in from an outside perspective.

I finally understand where she came from and how she chose not to break the cycle.

*I'm sorry, Mom.*

I'm sorry she was hurt so viciously as a child. It truly hurts to think about it, and I wish to be magical, to rescue the child she was, and to rescue my siblings and myself. We could have had such a different life. But the damage was too great. She did make a life in BC, though. She had Alvin, the Nuxalk tribe, and the village. She had surrogate daughters and grandchildren, and community members who loved the woman she presented to them. And she had us at the very end again: a full circle.

I close my journal, put it away, and think of my teen years, the voice inside, and how I, too, was fragmented. But I am here now, in 2002, only it feels like it could be 1976 or 1984 or 1998. Time, sound, light, DNA, all mixed with memory — mine, my mother's.

Time is fluid.

I can feel my younger self inside, and if it were possible, I'd pick up my five-year-old self and tell her she's going to be all right, that I've got her.

# EPILOGUE

IT TOOK ME SOME TIME to find the ground after my mother died. There was this imposed idea about the loss of a mother — the mythical mother — and the way I believed I was supposed to feel. In reality, I had long been motherless. Her death made it finite. It caused a shift in my life. It served as the end of something; it stopped the not knowing, the wondering, the what ifs.

*What if she denies everything?*

*What if she dies before I know why or what happened to her?*

*What if I crumble?*

Instead, I broke open, understood the root of my wounds, and I fed them as much light as I could find in order to heal.

My siblings and I eventually found our way to love. Yes, we struggled deeply — and sometimes we still do — but at the heart of it all is love.

There are now children, the next generation. Cycles of violence have been broken.

My father is still alive as I write this. He has been ill, and I've been to Montreal to see him, and even help him. He has denied ever hurting us, but I have learned to let it go. There's nothing for me to prove.

There were many days after my mother died when I remained inside my nest and wrote, painted, even tried to make music. I needed to be creative. Be alone. Be myself. To find a new reality.

It was during that time that Sharon Simone found me. She was searching for the actors who had worked on the TV movie about her life, *The Ultimate Betrayal*, which told the story of how she had survived her abusive FBI father and of the precedent-setting case in the States that she and her sisters had won.

Sharon had lost her daughter to a heroin overdose just before my mother died. We became comrades, friends. We achieved a lot together in the years that followed. We did anti-war work and spoke out about the invasion of Iraq, befriended a woman in the midst of war and helped her escape the Middle East. We also worked on child-abuse and anti-violence initiatives in Washington and other states. I founded a non-profit, Youth Out Loud, which raises awareness around child sexual abuse. Later, equal marriage rights became important to me. LGBTQ2+ people deserved equal access under the law. Period. I showed up to protest against groups such as Focus on the Family. I gave speeches at demonstrations and rallies, was thrown down the stairs at Queen's Park by police officers wearing gloves because they assumed we all had AIDS. Those days and the struggle for child-abuse awareness and equity issues propelled me forward.

I would still be rendered non-existent on the pages of screenplays. Things are slowly changing, however, with increased awareness of LGBTQ2+ people in the culture, but it is still primarily a white, heterosexual domain, controlled by powerful men. I understood that I needed to write my way out of my life, and in many ways, the writing saved me. Writing a book became the goal, and I would not let that slip away, because I understood it was far bigger than me.

I needed the silence. The page and pen became my friends, my confidantes, my soft place. It would be the one place where my thoughts, voice, politics, ideology, and identity could exist freely.

I believe that I will be okay. I believe that using my life for the purpose of helping others matters. That creating space and being okay within my own skin matter — being authentic and vocal, emotional and present, trying new things, and even if I fail, getting up to try again. And if I am lucky, I will learn many lessons and rise to as many occasions as present themselves. What exists in me now is the belief that I can make a difference, that my story and life experiences have value. I have much more to do in the world. Art, writing, poetry, music, film, and self-expression matter.

In my deepest place, I go to gratitude and love. It's love and hope that keep me motivated, the idea that there is so much more out there. And there are so many young people who have it right, like the Parkland students and young feminists and intersectional queer kids who are ahead of my generation culturally and polit-ically, who are invested in the equity of race and gender, of embrac-ing our differences, and of helping the planet and changing the world. So many beautiful souls.

It is impossible to continue without mentioning the Me Too movement and the women who are bringing awareness to sexual violence and rape. Brave women such as Anita Hill and Dr. Christine Blasey Ford, and, in Canada, women like Lucy DeCoutere — warriors who stand up in the face of hatred and fear and speak out regardless.

Historically, there has always been backlash against women who stand up and against any movement that threatens the power of those who hold it, that tries to right the wrongs of oppression: misogyny, racism, homophobia.

We will win these battles one day. We need to believe that.

As writer and civil rights activist Audre Lorde said, "Revolution is not a one-time event."

A century of feminist work preceded the Me Too move-ment, through the work of civil rights activists and other brave individuals who fought for freedom and equity. I am inspired by the activism of the founder of the Me Too movement, Tarana Burke, and Heather Heyer, the young woman who was killed in Charlottesville while protesting against neo-Nazis. I am inspired by ancestors and elders such as Harvey Milk; Edie Windsor; Alice Miller; Audre Lorde; Gloria Steinem; Maya Angelou; June Callwood; Martin Luther King Jr.; Stormé DeLarverie, Marsha P. Johnson, and all the Stonewall rioters of the 1960s; Oprah Winfrey; and Ruth Bader Ginsburg. And of people in my industry, current trailblazers that include Jill Soloway, Ellen DeGeneres, Ellen Page, and Lena Waithe. And I am inspired to continue the fight by the many LGBTQ2+ people who were taken from us too soon: Matthew Shepard, Brandon Teena, the victims at the Pulse nightclub in Orlando, and countless others. And by the dedicated people who contribute to the cause of equality through activism, by speaking up and engaging others in the conversation, by creating art and literature and film that reflects the world we live in. And to those who live in extreme danger in countries where it is a crime to be gay, I thank them for their bravery.

My friend Steffin died before he had a chance to read this book, but I knew he was with me throughout the process. He would be proud. He would flip his long hair and drink too much and dance with me if he were here. I cherish what was, cradle those moments shared, now a part of me, his story part of mine.

I couldn't do anything as a child to change my circumstances, but I am able to speak now, to write about it and share my experience. I am finally able to find all the words I wasn't able to then. This is my truth. And I hope it serves to help others.

# ACKNOWLEDGEMENTS

I WANT TO FIRST THANK my extraordinary friend and supporter, writer Diane Terrana. I am deeply grateful for your years of support through my writing life. Thank you also to my literary agent, Sam Hiyate at the Rights Factory, who gave my memoir a chance. I can't thank you enough.

Thanks to my publisher, Dundurn Press, and specifically to editorial director Kathryn Lane, my amazing and gracious developmental editor Allison Hirst, gracious project editor Elena Radic, copy editor Susan Fitzgerald, proofreader Dawn Hunter, publicists Tabassum Siddiqui and Michelle Melski, marketing associate Kathryn Bassett, artistic director Laura Boyle, and designer David Drummond. Special thanks go to acquisitions editor and publisher Scott Fraser for selecting my memoir and believing in it. It meant the world to me.

Thank you to friends and teachers and to everyone who agreed to read early drafts and provided feedback and endorsements.

I am forever grateful to my mentor from the Diaspora Dialogues Mentoring Program, David Layton, who gave me many months of his time and heart. I am also forever grateful to lifelong friend

Sharon Simone, Susie Vannicola, Dino Vannicola, Sharon Corder, Jack Blum, Holly Dale, Tanya Cinelli, Kate McKenzie, Joanna Holt, Christine Barker, Wendy Crewson, Aaron Martin, Patti McGillicuddy, Roland Emmerich, Denys Arcand, Helen Shaver, Hazel McGuiness, Anne Meara, Cynthia Dale, Marc Glassman, Colin Mochrie, Linda Riley, Farzana Doctor, Maggie Cassella, and Lorraine Segato for their support. Thanks also to Theresa Tova for being an ally. I would also like to thank the Diaspora Dialogues Charitable Society, Lit Up, the Ontario Arts Council, the Creative Writing Certificate Program at the University of Toronto, Pennant Media Group, and Sarah Kate Ellis of GLAAD. Much appreciation also goes to my manager, Gayle Abrams, for her support. Thanks to Deena, Nora, Jennifer, Kathy, Abby, Michele, Barbara, David, Richard, Pat, Wendy, Codi, Pheonix, Billy, Baby, and Laura for all the love and support along the path, from small acts of kindness to years of connection — it all mattered.

Thanks to all the women of Me Too and Time's Up and all the warriors who champion the intersectional rights of children, women, and queers. And to all LGBTQ2+ pioneers who came before me, who gave their lives and their love in the hope of making the world a better place, thank you, thank you, thank you.

Many names and dates in *All We Knew But Couldn't Say* have been changed. This book represents my account of what happened. Memories are individual, and we all process things differently in our minds and our hearts. This is a book about my experiences and is not meant to reflect the memories of others. With respect and love.

**Book Credits**

Acquiring Editor: Scott Fraser
Developmental Editor: Allison Hirst
Project Editor: Elena Radic
Copy Editor: Susan Fitzgerald
Proofreader: Dawn Hunter

Cover Designer: David Drummond
Interior Designer: Laura Boyle